quick
food

quick
food

LAUREL
GLEN
San Diego, California

Contents

Pot

Beef and chili bean soup

1 tablespoon vegetable oil
1 red onion, finely chopped
2 cloves garlic, crushed
2½ teaspoons chili flakes
2½ teaspoons ground cumin
2½ tablespoons finely chopped
  cilantro root and stem
1½ teaspoons ground coriander
1 lb. lean ground beef
1 tablespoon tomato paste
4 tomatoes, peeled, seeded,
  and diced
14-oz. can red kidney beans,
  drained and rinsed
8 cups beef stock
3 tablespoons chopped cilantro
  leaves
⅓ cup sour cream

Heat the oil in a large saucepan over medium heat. Cook the onion for 2–3 minutes or until softened. Add the garlic, chili flakes, cumin, cilantro, and coriander, and cook for 1 minute. Add the ground beef and cook for 3–4 minutes or until cooked through. Break up any lumps with a spoon.

Add the tomato paste, tomatoes, beans, and stock to the saucepan and bring to a boil. Reduce the heat and simmer for 15–20 minutes or until rich and reduced slightly. Remove any impurities on the surface. Stir in the chopped cilantro. Serve with the sour cream.

Serves 4

Scallops with soba noodles and dashi broth

8 oz. soba noodles
3 tablespoons mirin
¼ cup soy sauce
2 teaspoons rice wine vinegar
1 teaspoon dashi granules
2 scallions, sliced diagonally
1 teaspoon finely chopped
　fresh ginger
24 large scallops (without roe)
5 fresh cloud ear mushrooms,
　chopped
1 sheet nori, shredded, to garnish

Cook the soba noodles in a large saucepan of rapidly boiling water for 5 minutes or until tender. Drain and rinse under cold water.

Place the mirin, soy sauce, rice wine vinegar, dashi granules, and 3 cups water in a saucepan. Bring to a boil, then reduce the heat and simmer for 3–4 minutes. Add the scallions and ginger and keep at a gentle simmer until needed.

Heat a ridged cast-iron grill pan until very hot, and sear the scallops on both sides, in batches, for 1 minute.

Divide the noodles and cloud ear mushrooms among four deep serving bowls. Pour ¾ cup broth into each bowl and top each with 6 scallops. Garnish with the nori and serve immediately.

Serves 4

Note: If you can't buy fresh cloud ear mushrooms, use dried instead, but soak in warm water for 15–20 minutes before use.

Spaghettini with asparagus and arugula

½ cup extra-virgin olive oil
16 thin asparagus spears, cut
   into 2-in. pieces
12 oz. spaghettini
4 handfuls arugula, shredded
2 small fresh red chilies,
   finely chopped
2 teaspoons finely grated lemon zest
1 clove garlic, finely chopped
1 cup grated Parmesan
2 tablespoons lemon juice

Bring a large saucepan of water to a boil over medium heat. Add 1 tablespoon of the oil and a pinch of salt to the water and blanch the asparagus for 3–4 minutes. Remove the asparagus with a slotted spoon, rinse under cold water, drain, and place in a bowl. Return the water to a rapid boil and add the spaghettini. Cook the pasta until al dente. Drain and return to the saucepan.

Meanwhile, add the arugula, chilies, lemon zest, garlic, and ⅔ cup of the Parmesan to the asparagus and mix well. Add to the pasta, pour on the lemon juice and remaining olive oil, and season with salt and freshly ground black pepper. Stir well to evenly coat the pasta with the mixture. Divide among four pasta bowls, top with the remaining Parmesan, and serve.

Serves 4

Note: You can use other types of pasta, such as tagliatelle, macaroni, or spiral-shaped pasta.

Orecchiette with mushrooms, pancetta, and smoked mozzarella

13 oz. orecchiette
2 tablespoons extra-virgin olive oil
5 oz. sliced pancetta, cut into
  short thin strips
2¼ cups button mushrooms,
  sliced
2 leeks, sliced
1 cup whipping cream
6 oz. smoked mozzarella, cut into
  ½-in. cubes
8 fresh basil leaves, roughly torn

Cook the orecchiette in a large saucepan of rapidly boiling salted water until al dente.

Meanwhile, heat the oil in a large frying pan and sauté the pancetta, mushrooms, and leek over medium-high heat for 5 minutes. Stir in the cream and season with pepper—the pancetta should provide enough salty flavor. Simmer over low heat for 5 minutes or until the pasta is ready. Drain the pasta and stir into the frying pan. Add the mozzarella and basil and toss lightly.

Serves 4

Note: If you are watching your weight, you can use half chicken stock and half cream instead of all cream. Smoked provolone can be used instead of the mozzarella, if preferred.

Beef and red wine stew

2 lbs. diced beef
¼ cup seasoned all-purpose flour
1 tablespoon vegetable oil
5 oz. bacon, diced
8 bulb scallions, greens trimmed
   to ¾ in.
2¼ cups button mushrooms
2 cups red wine
2 tablespoons tomato paste
2 cups beef stock
1 bouquet garni

Toss the beef in the seasoned flour until evenly coated, shaking off any excess. Heat the oil in a large saucepan over high heat. Cook the beef in three batches for about 3 minutes or until well browned all over, adding a little extra oil as needed. Remove from the saucepan.

Add the bacon to the saucepan and cook for 2 minutes or until browned. Remove with a slotted spoon and add to the beef. Add the scallions and mushrooms and cook for 5 minutes or until the onions are browned. Remove from the saucepan.

Slowly pour the red wine into the saucepan, scraping up any sediment from the bottom with a wooden spoon. Stir in the tomato paste and stock. Add the bouquet garni and return the beef, bacon, and any juices to the saucepan. Bring to a boil, reduce the heat, and simmer for 45 minutes, then return the scallions and mushrooms to the saucepan. Cook for 1 hour or until the meat is very tender and the sauce is glossy. Serve with steamed new potatoes or mashed potatoes.

Serves 4

Note: Although this stew takes a long time to cook, it is very quick to prepare and the result is delicious.

Pea, lettuce, and bacon soup

2 tablespoons vegetable oil
2 onions, finely chopped
7 oz. bacon strips, chopped
2 lbs. frozen baby peas, defrosted
6 cups chicken stock
2½ lbs. iceberg lettuce,
  finely shredded
watercress sprigs, to garnish

Heat the oil in a large saucepan over medium heat. Add the onions and bacon and cook for 2–3 minutes or until soft, but not browned. Add the peas, stock, and half the lettuce to the saucepan, then simmer for 5 minutes. Season.

Allow the soup to cool slightly, then blend in batches until smooth. Return to the saucepan with the remaining lettuce and stir over medium-low heat until warmed through. Serve garnished with the watercress.

Serves 4

Lemon thyme tuna with tagliatelle

12 oz. tagliatelle
1/2 cup extra-virgin olive oil
1 small fresh red chili, seeded
  and finely chopped
1/4 cup drained capers
1 1/2 tablespoons fresh lemon thyme
  leaves
1 lb. tuna steaks, trimmed and
  cut into 1 1/4-in. cubes
1/4 cup lemon juice
1 tablespoon grated lemon zest
1/2 cup chopped fresh Italian parsley

Cook the tagliatelle in a large saucepan of rapidly boiling salted water until al dente. Drain, then return to the saucepan.

Meanwhile, heat 1 tablespoon of the oil in a large frying pan. Add the chili and capers and cook, stirring, for 1 minute or until the capers are crisp. Add the thyme and cook for another minute. Transfer to a bowl.

Heat another tablespoon of oil in the pan. Add the tuna cubes and toss for 2–3 minutes or until evenly browned on the outside but still pink in the center—check with the point of a sharp knife. Remove from the heat.

Add the tuna to the caper mixture along with the lemon juice, lemon zest, parsley, and the remaining oil, stirring gently until combined. Toss through the pasta, season with freshly ground black pepper, and serve immediately.

Serves 4

Creamy garlic shrimp fettuccine

13 oz. fresh fettuccine
1 tablespoon extra-virgin olive oil
1 onion, finely chopped
3 cloves garlic, crushed
13 oz. tomatoes, seeded and
  chopped
1/4 cup white wine
1 1/4 cups whipping cream
2 lbs. medium shrimp, peeled,
  deveined, and tails intact
1/2 cup loosely packed, roughly
  chopped fresh basil

Cook the fettuccine in a large saucepan of rapidly boiling salted water until al dente. Drain, then return to the saucepan.

Heat the oil in a large frying pan over medium-high heat and cook the onion and garlic, stirring, for 4–5 minutes or until the onion is soft. Add the tomatoes and wine and cook for 3 minutes before adding the cream. Bring to a boil, then reduce the heat to medium-low and simmer for 5 minutes or until the mixture slightly thickens. Stir in the shrimp, then simmer for 3–4 minutes or until the shrimp turn pink and are curled and cooked through. Toss with the pasta, gently stir in the basil, season, and serve immediately.

Serves 4

Beef masala with coconut rice

1 tablespoon vegetable oil
2 lbs. beef chuck, trimmed and cut
   into $3/4$-in. cubes
1 large onion, thinly sliced
3 cloves garlic, chopped
$1/3$ cup tikka masala curry paste
2 teaspoons tamarind concentrate
$3^1/4$ cups coconut milk
4 fresh curry leaves
$1^1/2$ cups jasmine rice

Heat the oil in a large saucepan over high heat. Add the meat and cook in three batches for 4 minutes per batch, or until evenly browned.

Reduce the heat to medium, add the onion to the saucepan, cook for 5 minutes, add the garlic, and cook for 1 minute. Stir in the curry paste and tamarind for 30–60 seconds or until fragrant. Return the beef to the saucepan, add $2^1/4$ cups coconut milk and the curry leaves, and bring to a boil. Reduce the heat and simmer gently for $1^1/2$ hours or until the meat is tender and the sauce has reduced. Add some water if the sauce starts to stick to the bottom of the saucepan.

Meanwhile, to make the coconut rice, wash and thoroughly drain the rice. Put the rice, the remaining coconut milk, and 1 cup water in a saucepan and bring slowly to a boil, stirring constantly. Boil for 1 minute, then reduce the heat to low and cook, covered tightly, for 20 minutes. Remove from the heat and leave, covered, for 10 minutes. Fluff the rice with a fork before serving. To serve, season to taste and remove the curry leaves, if desired. Serve with the rice.

Serves 4

Note: Beef masala takes a while to cook but the preparation time is short.

Spaghetti marinara

2 tablespoons extra-virgin olive oil
1 onion, finely chopped
2 cloves garlic, crushed
2 14-oz. cans diced tomatoes
1/4 cup tomato paste
1 lb. spaghetti
1 lb. seafood medley (see Note)
8 mussels, beards removed,
    scrubbed
2 tablespoons shredded fresh basil

Heat the oil in a saucepan over medium heat, add the onion, and cook for 5 minutes or until soft and golden. Add the garlic and stir for 1 minute or until aromatic. Add the tomatoes and tomato paste and bring to a boil, then reduce the heat and simmer for 20–25 minutes or until the sauce becomes rich and pulpy. Stir the sauce occasionally during cooking. Season with salt and cracked black pepper. Meanwhile, cook the spaghetti in a large saucepan of rapidly boiling water until al dente. Drain well, return to the saucepan, and keep warm.

Add the seafood mix and the mussels to the tomato sauce, and cook for 2–3 minutes or until the seafood is cooked and the mussels are open. Discard any mussels that don't open. Stir in the basil. Toss the sauce through the warm pasta and serve.

Serves 4–6

Note: Seafood medley—mixed seafood—is available in many supermarkets. Alternatively, make your own by buying different types of seafood, such as octopus, fish fillets, and squid, and chopping each into bite-size pieces.

Buckwheat noodles with sweet and sour peppers

3 peppers (preferably red, green,
   and yellow)
2 tablespoons vegetable oil
5 teaspoons sesame oil
2 star anise
1/4 cup red wine vinegar
1 tablespoon fish sauce
1/2 cup sugar
10 oz. buckwheat noodles
1/2 tablespoon balsamic vinegar
1/2 teaspoon sugar, extra
2 scallions, finely sliced
2 tablespoons sesame seeds,
   lightly toasted

Thinly slice the peppers. Heat the vegetable oil and 1 teaspoon sesame oil in a saucepan over medium heat and cook the star anise for 1 minute or until the oil begins to smoke. Add the peppers and stir for 2 minutes. Reduce the heat to low and cook, covered, for 5 minutes, stirring occasionally. Increase to medium heat and add the vinegar, fish sauce, and sugar, stirring until dissolved. Boil for 2 minutes, then remove from the heat and cool. Remove the star anise. Drain and place the peppers in a bowl.

Cook the noodles in a large saucepan of rapidly boiling water for 5 minutes. Drain and rinse.

Combine the balsamic vinegar, remaining sesame oil, extra sugar, and 1/2 teaspoon salt, stirring until the sugar dissolves. Add the noodles and toss to coat, then combine with the peppers and scallions. Sprinkle with the sesame seeds and serve.

Serves 4

Szechuan chicken

1/4 teaspoon five-spice powder
1 1/2 lbs. boneless chicken thighs,
  halved
2 tablespoons peanut oil
1 tablespoon julienned fresh ginger
1 teaspoon Szechuan peppercorns,
  crushed
1 teaspoon chili bean paste
  (*toban jian*)
2 tablespoons light soy sauce
1 tablespoon Chinese rice wine
1 1/4 cups jasmine rice
1 1/4 lbs. baby bok choy,
  leaves separated

Sprinkle the five-spice powder over the chicken. Heat a saucepan or wok until very hot, add half the oil, and swirl to coat. Add the chicken and cook for 2 minutes on each side or until browned. Remove from the wok.

Reduce the heat to medium and cook the ginger for 30 seconds. Add the peppercorns and chili bean paste. Return the chicken to the pan or wok, add the soy sauce, wine, and 1/2 cup water, then simmer for 15–20 minutes or until cooked.

Meanwhile, add the rice to a large saucepan of rapidly boiling water and cook for 12 minutes, stirring occasionally. Drain well.

Heat the remaining oil in a saucepan. Add the bok choy and toss for 1 minute or until the leaves wilt and the stems are tender. Serve with the chicken and rice.

Serves 4

Ziti carbonara

1 lb. ziti
1 tablespoon extra-virgin olive oil
6½-oz. piece pancetta, cut into
    long, thin strips
4 egg yolks
1¼ cups whipping cream
½ cup grated Parmesan
2 tablespoons finely chopped
    fresh Italian parsley

Cook the pasta in a large saucepan of rapidly boiling salted water until al dente. Drain well and return to the saucepan. Meanwhile, heat the olive oil in a nonstick frying pan and cook the pancetta over high heat for 6 minutes or until crisp and golden.

Beat the egg yolks, cream, and Parmesan together in a bowl and season generously. Pour over the hot pasta in the saucepan and toss gently. Add the pancetta and parsley. Return the saucepan to very low heat and cook for 30–60 seconds or until the sauce has thickened and coats the pasta. Don't cook over high heat or the eggs will scramble. Season with salt and freshly ground black pepper, and serve immediately with extra Parmesan, if desired.

Serves 4–6

Pasta with pork and fennel sausages

6 Italian pork and fennel sausages
  (about 1 lb. 2 oz.)
1 tablespoon extra-virgin olive oil
1 small red onion, finely chopped
2–3 cloves garlic, crushed
½ teaspoon chili flakes
10 oz. button mushrooms,
  thinly sliced
2 14-oz. cans diced tomatoes
1 tablespoon finely chopped
  fresh thyme
1 lb. penne rigate
grated Parmesan, to serve

Split the sausages open, remove and crumble the filling, and discard the skins.

Heat the oil in a large saucepan over medium-high heat and cook the onion for 3–4 minutes or until fragrant and transparent. Add the garlic, chili flakes, mushrooms, and crumbled sausage meat. Cook over high heat, stirring gently to mash the sausage meat, for 4–5 minutes or until the meat is evenly browned. If necessary, use a spoon to remove any excess fat from the saucepan, leaving about a tablespoon of oil. Continue to cook, stirring once or twice, for 10 minutes.

Stir in the tomatoes and thyme, then bring the sauce to a boil. Cover and cook over medium-low heat for 20 minutes, stirring occasionally to make sure the sauce doesn't stick to the bottom of the saucepan.

Meanwhile, cook the penne rigate in a large saucepan of rapidly boiling salted water until al dente. Drain well, then add to the sauce, stirring to combine. Garnish with Parmesan, then serve immediately with a green salad.

Serves 4

Note: This dish takes a while to cook, but the ingredients won't take too long to prepare.

Cotelli with spring vegetables

1 lb. cotelli or rotelle pasta
2 cups frozen peas
2 cups frozen fava beans, blanched
and peeled
1/3 cup extra-virgin olive oil
6 scallions, cut into 1 1/4-in. pieces
2 cloves garlic, finely chopped
1 cup chicken stock
12 thin, fresh asparagus spears,
cut into 2-in. pieces
1 lemon

Cook the cotelli in a large saucepan of rapidly boiling salted water until al dente. Drain and return to the saucepan. Meanwhile, cook the peas in a saucepan of boiling water for 1–2 minutes, until tender. Remove with a slotted spoon and plunge into cold water. Add the fava beans to the saucepan, cook for 1–2 minutes, then drain and plunge into cold water. Remove and slip the skins off.

Heat 2 tablespoons of the oil in a frying pan. Add the scallions and garlic and cook over medium heat for 2 minutes or until softened. Pour in the stock and cook for 5 minutes or until slightly reduced. Add the asparagus and cook for 3–4 minutes, until bright green and just tender. Stir in the peas and fava beans and cook for 2–3 minutes or until heated through.

Toss the remaining oil through the pasta, then add the vegetable mixture, 1/2 teaspoon finely grated lemon zest, and 1/4 cup lemon juice. Season to taste with salt and cracked black pepper, and toss together well. Divide among four bowls and top with shaved Parmesan, if desired.

Serves 4

Paprika veal with caraway noodles

3 tablespoons vegetable oil
2 lbs. diced veal shoulder
1 large onion, thinly sliced
3 cloves garlic, finely chopped
1/4 cup Hungarian paprika
1/2 teaspoon caraway seeds
2 14-oz. cans diced tomatoes, one
  can drained
11 oz. fresh fettuccine
1 3/4 tablespoons butter, softened

Heat half the oil in a large saucepan over medium-high heat, then brown the veal in batches for 3 minutes per batch. Remove the veal from the pan and set aside with any pan juices.

Add the remaining oil to the saucepan and sauté the onion and garlic over medium heat for 5 minutes or until softened. Add the paprika and 1/4 teaspoon of the caraway seeds and stir for 30 seconds.

Add the diced tomatoes and their liquid, plus 1/2 cup water. Return the veal to the saucepan with any juices, increase the heat to high, and bring to a boil. Reduce the heat to low, then cover and simmer for 1 hour 15 minutes or until the meat is tender and the sauce has thickened.

About 15 minutes before the veal is ready, cook the pasta in a large saucepan of rapidly boiling salted water until al dente. Drain, then return to the saucepan. Stir in the butter and the remaining caraway seeds. Serve immediately with the veal.

Serves 4

Note: Although this recipe has a long cooking time, it is quick to prepare.

Tomato ditalini soup

2 tablespoons extra-virgin olive oil
1 large onion, finely chopped
2 celery stalks, finely chopped
3 vine-ripened tomatoes
6 cups chicken or vegetable stock
½ cup ditalini
2 tablespoons chopped fresh
   Italian parsley

Heat the oil in a large saucepan over medium heat. Add the onion and celery and cook for 5 minutes or until they have softened.

Score a cross in the bottom of each tomato, then place them in a bowl of boiling water for 1 minute. Plunge into cold water and peel the skin away from the cross. Halve the tomatoes and scoop out the seeds. Roughly chop the flesh. Add the stock and tomatoes to the onion mixture and bring to a boil. Add the ditalini and cook for 10 minutes or until al dente. Season and sprinkle with parsley. Serve with crusty bread.

Serves 4

Cheese tortellini with pepper and almond sauce

1 red pepper
1 yellow pepper
2/3 cup sliced almonds
8 scallions
2 cloves garlic, crushed
1 lb. cheese tortellini
2/3 cup extra-virgin olive oil
1/3 cup finely grated pecorino cheese

Cut the peppers into large pieces, removing the seeds and membrane. Place, skin-side up, under a preheated broiler until the skin blackens and blisters. Cool in a plastic bag, then peel away the skin. Spread the almonds on a cookie sheet and toast for 1–2 minutes or until lightly toasted.

Roughly chop the white part of the scallions and slice the green tops, setting them aside for garnish. Put the peppers, almonds, garlic, and white part of the scallions in a food processor and pulse until chopped.

Cook the pasta in a large saucepan of boiling water until al dente. Drain and return to the saucepan. Toss the pepper mixture through the pasta, then add the oil and cheese. Season to taste. Serve garnished with the green scallion slices.

Serves 4

Fresh tomato and basil sauce with pasta

13 oz. spaghetti
5 tablespoons extra-virgin olive oil
5 cloves garlic, thinly sliced
6 vine-ripened tomatoes, seeded
  and chopped
3/4 cup torn fresh basil leaves
grated Parmesan, for serving

Bring a large saucepan of water to a boil, add a pinch of salt, then add the pasta and cook according to the packet instructions until al dente. Drain the pasta. If the pasta will be sitting around for a little while before being added to the sauce, return it to the saucepan and toss through a little olive oil to keep it from sticking together.

While the pasta is cooking, heat 4 tablespoons of the oil in a frying pan and cook the garlic over low heat for 1 minute. As soon as the garlic begins to change color, remove the pan from the heat and add the remaining oil.

Add the cooked pasta to the saucepan with the tomatoes and basil. Season generously with salt and freshly ground black pepper. Toss well and serve drizzled with a little extra-virgin olive oil and sprinkled with grated Parmesan.

Serves 4

Veal pasta with alfredo sauce

1 1/4 lbs. veal-filled pasta
1/3 cup butter
1 1/2 cups grated Parmesan
1 1/4 cups whipping cream
2 tablespoons chopped
    fresh marjoram

Cook the veal pasta in a large saucepan of rapidly boiling salted water until al dente. Drain and return to the saucepan.

Just before the pasta is cooked, melt the butter in a saucepan over low heat. Add the Parmesan and cream and bring to a boil. Reduce the heat and simmer, stirring constantly, for 2 minutes or until the sauce has thickened slightly. Stir in the marjoram and season with salt and cracked black pepper. Toss the sauce through the pasta. Serve immediately.

Serves 4–6

Note: Any fresh herb, such as parsley, thyme, chervil, or dill, can be used instead of marjoram.

Thai green chicken curry with cilantro rice

1¼ cups jasmine rice
1 tablespoon vegetable oil
1–2 tablespoons Thai green
  curry paste
4 fresh kaffir lime leaves
1 tablespoon fish sauce
2 teaspoons palm sugar or
  brown sugar
14-oz. can coconut cream
1½ lbs. skinless, boneless
  chicken breasts, cut into strips
  (³/₄ x 2½ in.)
4 tablespoons roughly chopped
  cilantro leaves
2 tablespoons whole cilantro leaves

Bring a large saucepan of water to a boil. Add the rice and cook for 12 minutes, stirring occasionally. Drain well.

Meanwhile, heat the oil over high heat in a saucepan or wok, then add the curry paste and lime leaves and fry over medium-high heat for 1–2 minutes or until fragrant. Add the fish sauce and sugar and mix well. Pour in the coconut cream, bring to a boil, then add the chicken strips. Reduce the heat to medium and simmer for 12–15 minutes or until the sauce is reduced and the chicken is tender and cooked.

Just before serving, stir the chopped cilantro through the rice. Serve the curry over the cilantro rice and garnish with cilantro leaves.

Serves 4

Chicken and spinach risoni soup

1 tablespoon extra-virgin olive oil
1 leek, quartered lengthwise and
  thinly sliced
2 cloves garlic, crushed
1 teaspoon ground cumin
6 cups chicken stock
2 skinless, boneless chicken breasts
  (about 1 lb.)
1 cup risoni
5 oz. baby spinach leaves, roughly
  chopped
1 tablespoon chopped fresh dill
2 teaspoons lemon juice

Heat the oil in a large saucepan over low heat. Add the leek and cook for 8–10 minutes or until soft. Add the garlic and cumin and cook for 1 minute. Pour the stock into the saucepan, increase the heat to high, and bring to a boil. Reduce the heat to low, add the chicken breasts, and simmer, covered, for 8 minutes. Remove the chicken from the broth, allow to cool slightly, then shred.

Stir the risoni into the broth and simmer for 12 minutes or until al dente.

Return the chicken to the broth along with the spinach and dill. Simmer for 2 minutes or until the spinach has wilted. Stir in the lemon juice, season to taste with salt and freshly ground black pepper, and serve.

Serves 4

Beef in black bean sauce

4 tablespoons canned, salted black
  beans in soy sauce
1½ lbs. beef rump steak
1 tablespoon peanut oil
1 tablespoon sesame oil
1 large onion, thinly sliced
1 clove garlic, finely chopped
1½ x ½-in. piece fresh ginger, peeled
  and finely chopped
1 small, fresh red chili, finely chopped
2 teaspoons cornstarch
2 tablespoons dark soy sauce
1 teaspoon sugar
¼ cup beef stock
1 scallion, thinly sliced diagonally,
  to garnish

Rinse and then soak the black beans
in cold water for 5 minutes. Drain
and roughly mash the beans with a
fork. Trim the beef of all fat and sinew,
then cut the meat in thin slices across
the grain.

Heat a saucepan over medium heat
and add half each of the peanut and
sesame oils. Add the beef in two
batches and stir each for 2 minutes or
until well browned. Transfer the beef
and any liquid to a bowl. Heat the
remaining oils, add the onion, and stir
for 2 minutes. Add the garlic, ginger,
and chili and stir for 1 minute.

Mix the cornstarch with 1 teaspoon
water, then return the beef and any
cooking liquid to the saucepan with
the black beans, soy sauce, sugar,
stock, and cornstarch paste. Stir for
1–2 minutes or until the sauce boils
and thickens. Garnish with the
scallions and serve with steamed rice.

Serves 4

Spaghetti Niçoise

11 oz. spaghetti
8 quail eggs (or 4 chicken eggs)
3 6-oz. cans tuna in oil
⅓ cup pitted and halved Kalamata
  olives
⅔ cup sun-dried tomatoes,
  halved lengthwise
4 anchovy fillets, chopped into
  small pieces
1 teaspoon finely grated lemon zest
2 tablespoons lemon juice
3 tablespoons baby capers, drained
3 tablespoons chopped fresh
  Italian parsley

Cook the pasta in a large saucepan of rapidly boiling salted water until al dente. Meanwhile, place the eggs in a saucepan of cold water, bring to a boil, and cook for 4 minutes (10 minutes for chicken eggs). Drain, cool under cold water, then peel. Halve the quail eggs or quarter the chicken eggs.

Empty the tuna and its oil into a large bowl. Add the olives, tomato halves, anchovies, lemon zest and juice, capers, and 2 tablespoons of the parsley. Drain the pasta and rinse in a little cold water, then toss gently through the tuna mixture. Divide among serving bowls, garnish with egg and the remaining parsley, and serve.

Serves 4–6

Penne with squash, baked ricotta, and prosciutto

1 lb. penne
15 oz. butternut squash,
  cut into ½-in. cubes
¼ cup extra-virgin olive oil
2 cloves garlic, crushed
3½ oz. sun-dried tomatoes, chopped
4 slices prosciutto, chopped
8 oz. baked ricotta, cut into
  ½-in. cubes
3 tablespoons shredded fresh basil

Cook the penne in a large saucepan of rapidly boiling salted water until al dente. Drain. Meanwhile, cook the squash in a saucepan of boiling water for 10–12 minutes or until just tender, then drain.

Heat the oil in a large saucepan, add the garlic, and cook over medium heat for 30 seconds. Add the tomatoes, prosciutto, squash, and penne and toss over low heat for 1–2 minutes or until heated through.

Add the baked ricotta and the basil, season with salt and cracked black pepper, and serve immediately.

Serves 4

Chicken, artichoke, and fava bean stew

1 cup frozen fava beans
8 chicken thighs, bone in
1/2 cup seasoned all-purpose flour
2 tablespoons oil
1 large red onion, cut into small
  wedges
1/2 cup dry white wine
1 1/4 cups chicken stock
2 teaspoons finely chopped fresh
  rosemary
1 1/2 cups marinated artichokes,
  well drained and quartered
1 lb. 10 oz. potatoes, cut into large
  pieces
1/4 cup butter

Remove the skins from the fava beans. Coat the chicken in the flour, shaking off the excess. Heat the oil in a saucepan or flameproof casserole dish, then brown the chicken in two batches on all sides over medium heat. Remove and drain on crumpled paper towels.

Add the onion to the pan and cook for 3–4 minutes or until soft but not brown. Increase the heat to high, pour in the wine, and boil for 2 minutes or until reduced to a syrup. Stir in 1 cup of stock and bring just to a boil, then return the chicken to the pan with the rosemary. Reduce the heat to low and simmer, covered, for 45 minutes. Add the artichokes, increase the heat to high, and return to a boil. Reduce to a simmer and cook, uncovered, for 10–15 minutes. Add the beans and cook for 5 minutes.

Meanwhile, cook the potatoes in a saucepan of boiling water for 15–20 minutes or until tender. Drain, then return to the saucepan. Add the butter and the remaining stock and mash with a potato masher. Serve on the side.

Serves 4

Ricotta and mushroom lasagna

1 cup fresh ricotta
2/3 cup grated Parmesan
3 1/2 tablespoons extra-virgin olive oil
1 onion, thinly sliced
2 cloves garlic, crushed
1 lb. portobello mushrooms, sliced
1 1/4 cups tomato pasta sauce
6 sheets fresh lasagna, cut in half,
   then into 4 1/2-in. squares
1 cup baby spinach leaves, washed

Mix the ricotta with half the Parmesan and season well. Heat 2 tablespoons oil in a large frying pan, add the onion, and cook for 2 minutes or until it softens. Add the garlic and mushrooms and cook for 1–2 minutes or until the mushrooms start to soften. Add the tomato pasta sauce and cook for another 5–6 minutes or until the sauce starts to thicken. Season well.

Meanwhile, bring a deep saucepan of water to a boil and add 1 tablespoon oil and a pinch of salt. Cook the lasagna squares for 2–3 minutes. Drain, keeping each square separate. Put the spinach in a saucepan with just the water clinging to the leaves. Cover and cook over medium heat for 1–2 minutes or until the spinach has wilted.

To assemble, place a pasta square on each serving plate, then divide the mushroom sauce among the squares. Place another pasta square on top, then spread the ricotta mixture evenly over the surface, leaving a 3/4-in. border. Divide the spinach evenly among the four servings. Finally, place another pasta square on top, brush or drizzle with the remaining oil, then sprinkle with the remaining Parmesan. Season. Serve with a green salad and crusty bread.

Serves 4

Moroccan chicken

1 tablespoon Moroccan spice blend
1 lb. 10 oz. boneless chicken thighs,
    trimmed and halved
1 tablespoon vegetable oil
¼ cup butter
1 large onion, cut into wedges
1 cinnamon stick
2 cloves garlic, crushed
2 tablespoons lemon juice
1 cup chicken stock
⅓ cup pitted prunes, halved
1½ cups couscous
lemon wedges, for serving

Sprinkle half the spice blend over the chicken. Heat the oil and 1 tablespoon of the butter in a large saucepan or deep-sided frying pan over medium heat. Cook the chicken in two batches for 5 minutes or until evenly browned. Remove from the saucepan, then add the onion and cinnamon stick and cook for 2–3 minutes before adding the garlic. Return the chicken to the saucepan and add the lemon juice and the remaining spice blend. Season, then cook, covered, for 5 minutes.

Add the stock and prunes to the saucepan and bring to a boil. Reduce the heat to medium-low and cook, uncovered, for 15 minutes or until the chicken is cooked and the liquid has reduced to a sauce. Before serving, stir 1 tablespoon of the butter into the sauce.

About 10 minutes before the chicken is ready, place the couscous in a heatproof bowl, add 1½ cups boiling water, and allow to stand for 3–5 minutes. Stir in the remaining butter and fluff with a fork until the butter has melted and the grains separate. Serve with the chicken.

Serves 4

Tagliatelle with feta, tomatoes, and arugula

4 vine-ripened tomatoes
1 small red onion, finely chopped
4 tablespoons shredded fresh basil
2 tablespoons extra-virgin olive oil
12 oz. tagliatelle
2 cloves garlic, finely chopped
5 handfuls baby arugula leaves
1 cup soft feta, crumbled
1/4 cup fresh, small, whole basil leaves

Score a cross in the bottom of each tomato, then place in a bowl of boiling water for 1 minute. Plunge into cold water and peel the skin away from the cross. Cut in half and remove the seeds with a teaspoon. Chop, then transfer to a bowl. Add the onion and basil, stir in 1 tablespoon of the oil, and set aside.

Cook the pasta in a large saucepan of rapidly boiling salted water until al dente. Drain, reserving 1/2 cup of the water. Return the pasta to the pan, add the remaining oil, the garlic, and the reserved pasta water, and toss together over medium heat for 1–2 minutes to warm through. Stir in the tomato mixture, arugula, and feta. Season to taste with salt and pepper. Divide among four serving plates and serve immediately, garnished with the whole basil leaves.

Serves 4

Pasta with beef ragu

4 oz. bacon or pancetta
  (not trimmed), finely chopped
1 onion, finely chopped
3 cloves garlic, crushed
1 bay leaf
1 lb. 10 oz. lean ground beef
2 cups red wine
1/3 cup tomato paste
13 oz. tagliatelle
freshly grated Parmesan, to garnish

Heat a large, deep frying pan (preferably stainless steel or noncoated). Add the bacon or pancetta and cook over medium-high heat for 2 minutes or until soft and just starting to brown. Add the onion, garlic, and bay leaf and cook for 2 minutes or until the onion is soft and just starting to brown.

Add the ground beef and stir for 4 minutes or until the meat browns, breaking up any lumps with the back of a wooden spoon. Add the wine, tomato paste, and 1 cup water and stir well. Bring to a boil, then reduce the heat and simmer, covered, for 40 minutes. Remove the lid and cook for another 40 minutes or until reduced to a thick, glossy sauce.

Bring a large saucepan of salted water to a rapid boil 20 minutes before the ragu is ready, and cook the pasta until al dente. Drain. Serve the sauce over the pasta and garnish with a little grated Parmesan.

Serves 4

Note: This recipe is easily prepared, but it takes a while to cook.

Spaghetti bolognese

1 tablespoon extra-virgin olive oil
1 large onion, diced
2 cloves garlic, crushed
1¼ lbs. ground beef
½ cup red wine
½ cup beef stock
2 14-oz. cans diced tomatoes
1 carrot, grated
12 oz. spaghetti

Heat the oil over medium heat in a large saucepan, add the onion and garlic, and cook for 1–2 minutes or until soft. Add the beef and cook, stirring to break up any lumps, for 5 minutes or until the meat is browned. Pour in the wine and simmer for 2–3 minutes or until reduced slightly, then add the stock and simmer for another 2 minutes. Add the tomatoes and carrot and season well with salt and pepper. Cook over low heat for 40 minutes.

About 15 minutes before serving time, cook the pasta in a large saucepan of rapidly boiling salted water until al dente. Drain well and keep warm. Divide the pasta among four serving bowls and pour the meat sauce over the pasta. Garnish with parsley, if desired.

Serves 4

Note: This dish cooks for a long time but doesn't take long to prepare.

Coconut beef curry on turmeric rice

2 tablespoons vegetable oil
1 large onion, sliced
2 tablespoons vindaloo curry paste
2 lbs. chuck steak, trimmed and
  cubed
1 cup beef stock
3/4 cup coconut cream
1 1/4 cups basmati rice
3/4 teaspoon ground turmeric

Heat the oil in a large saucepan over medium-high heat. Add the onion and cook for 2–3 minutes or until starting to soften. Add the curry paste and stir for 1 minute or until fragrant. Add the steak and brown evenly for 5 minutes.

Pour in the stock and bring to a boil. Reduce the heat to very low and simmer, covered, for 1 hour or until the meat is tender. Uncover and cook for 15 minutes to reduce the sauce.

Add the coconut cream, return to a boil, then simmer over low heat for 15–20 minutes or until the beef is tender and the sauce has reduced.

Rinse the rice and place it in a large saucepan 25 minutes before the beef is ready. Add the turmeric and 1 3/4 cups water and bring to a boil. Reduce the heat to very low, then cook, covered, for 10 minutes. Remove from the heat and allow to rest, covered, for 10 minutes. Divide the rice among four wide serving bowls and top with the beef curry.

Serves 4

Note: Although this curry cooks for a long time, it is prepared very quickly.

Chicken and cider stew with mashed potatoes and apples

2 lbs. boneless chicken thighs,
  trimmed and cut into ³/₄-in. cubes
1½ tablespoons finely chopped
  fresh thyme
1 tablespoon vegetable oil
⅓ cup butter
3 shallots, thinly sliced
1½ cups apple cider
2 lbs. potatoes, cubed
2 large green apples, peeled,
  cored, and sliced into eight pieces
²/₃ cup cream

Season the chicken with salt and pepper and 2 teaspoons of the thyme. Heat the oil and 1 tablespoon of the butter in a large saucepan over medium heat. Brown the chicken in two batches for 2–3 minutes. Remove. Add the shallots and the remaining thyme to the saucepan and sauté for 2 minutes. Pour in the cider, then bring to a boil, scraping off any sediment from the bottom. Return the chicken to the saucepan and cover. Reduce the heat to medium-low and cook for 35–40 minutes or until the chicken is tender and the sauce has reduced (check occasionally to see if any water needs to be added).

Meanwhile, cook the potatoes and apples in a saucepan of boiling water for 15–20 minutes or until tender. Drain and return to the saucepan over low heat for a minute to allow any water to evaporate. Remove from the heat and mash with a potato masher. Stir in 2 tablespoons of the cream and the remaining butter with a wooden spoon, then season well.

Stir the remaining cream into the stew and cook for another 2–4 minutes or until the sauce has thickened. Serve at once with the mashed potatoes and apples and a crisp green salad.

Serves 4

Vegetable tagine with couscous

¼ cup extra-virgin olive oil
1 large red pepper, seeded
  and cut into quarters
1 large eggplant, sliced into
  ½-in. rounds, then halved
14-oz. can diced tomatoes
1 tablespoon harissa paste (see Note)
1 tablespoon Moroccan spice blend
1 cup vegetable stock
2 large zucchini, cut into ¾-in.
  chunks
1½ cups couscous
1 tablespoon butter

Heat 1 tablespoon of the oil in a saucepan over medium-high heat. Sauté the pepper, skin-side down, covered, for 3–4 minutes or until the skin is well browned. Remove from the saucepan. Peel, then cut the flesh into ½-in. slices. Heat the remaining oil in the saucepan and cook the eggplant in batches over medium-high heat for 4–5 minutes or until well browned.

Return the pepper to the saucepan, then stir in the tomatoes, harissa paste, and Moroccan spice blend. Pour in the stock and bring to a boil. Reduce the heat to medium-low and simmer, uncovered, for 15 minutes. Add the zucchini and eggplant and cook for another 8 minutes or until the vegetables are tender.

Place the couscous in a heatproof bowl 10 minutes before the vegetables are ready. Add 1½ cups boiling water and allow to rest for 3–5 minutes. Stir in the butter and fluff with a fork until the butter has melted and the grains separate. Serve the vegetable tagine with the couscous.

Serves 4

Note: Harissa, available at specialty food stores, is a blend of chilies, garlic, spices, and oil.

Tomato and basil mussels

½ cup dry white wine
2 bay leaves
2 lbs. mussels, scrubbed and beards
  removed
2 cups tomato pasta sauce
1–2 teaspoons sugar to taste
2 tablespoons extra-virgin olive oil
4 tablespoons shredded fresh basil
2 tablespoons snipped fresh chives

Place the wine and bay leaves in a large, wide saucepan and bring to a boil. Discard any broken mussels, add the rest to the saucepan, and cook, covered with a tight-fitting lid, over high heat for 4 minutes or until the mussels open.

Place the pasta sauce, sugar, oil, and basil in a bowl, and mix together well.

Discard any mussels that have not opened. Drain, reserving the cooking juices. Return the mussels to the saucepan, add the tomato mixture and ½ cup of the reserved cooking juices, and stir over high heat for 3–4 minutes or until warmed through. Sprinkle with chives and serve in warmed bowls with bread.

Serves 4

Fresh vegetable lasagna with arugula

Balsamic syrup
1/3 cup balsamic vinegar
1 1/2 tablespoons brown sugar

16 asparagus spears, trimmed and
    cut into 2-in. pieces
1 cup fresh or frozen peas
2 large zucchini, cut into thin ribbons
2 fresh lasagna sheets
    (each sheet 10 x 14 in.)
3 handfuls arugula leaves
1 cup fresh basil, torn
2 tablespoons extra-virgin olive oil
1 cup low-fat ricotta
1 cup sun-dried tomatoes
Parmesan shavings, to garnish

Stir the vinegar and brown sugar in a small saucepan over medium heat until the sugar dissolves. Reduce the heat and simmer for 3–4 minutes or until the sauce becomes syrupy. Remove from the heat.

Bring a large saucepan of salted water to a boil. Blanch the asparagus, peas and zucchini in separate batches until just tender, rinsing each batch in cold water. Return the cooking liquid to a boil. Cook the lasagna sheets in the boiling water for 1–2 minutes or until al dente. Rinse in cold water and drain well. Cut each sheet in half lengthwise.

Toss the vegetables and the arugula with the basil and olive oil. Season. To assemble, place one strip of pasta on a serving plate—a third of it on the center of the plate and two-thirds overhanging one side. Place a small amount of the salad on the middle third, topped with some ricotta and tomatoes. Season lightly and fold over a third of the lasagna sheet. Top with a layer of salad, ricotta, and tomatoes. Fold back the final layer of pasta and garnish with salad and tomatoes. Repeat with the remaining pasta, salad, ricotta, and tomatoes to make four. Drizzle with the balsamic syrup and garnish with Parmesan.

Serves 4

Farfalle with spinach and bacon

13 oz. farfalle
2 tablespoons extra-virgin olive oil
8 oz. bacon, chopped
1 red onion, finely chopped
8 oz. baby spinach leaves, stems
    trimmed
1–2 tablespoons sweet chili sauce
    (optional)
¼ cup crumbled goat feta

Cook the pasta in a large saucepan of rapidly boiling salted water until al dente, then drain and return to the saucepan. Meanwhile, heat the oil in a frying pan, add the bacon, and cook over medium heat for 3 minutes or until golden. Add the onion and cook for another 4 minutes or until softened. Toss the spinach leaves through the onion and bacon mixture for 30 seconds or until just wilted.

Add the bacon and spinach mixture to the drained pasta, then stir in the sweet chili sauce. Season to taste with salt and cracked black pepper and toss well. Spoon into warm bowls and sprinkle with the crumbled feta. Serve immediately.

Serves 4

Madras lamb pilaf

1/4 cup vegetable oil
2 onions, thinly sliced
1 cup plain yogurt
1/4 cup Madras curry paste
2 cups basmati rice, well rinsed
8 large French-trimmed lamb chops
4 tablespoons chopped fresh mint
1/2 cup slivered almonds,
  lightly toasted

Heat 2 tablespoons of the oil in a large saucepan, add the onions, and cook over medium heat for 4–5 minutes or until soft. Remove half with a slotted spoon, set aside, and keep warm. Add 3/4 cup of the yogurt and 2 tablespoons of the curry paste to the saucepan. Cook, stirring, for 2 minutes. Stir in the rice until well coated. Pour in 2 cups water, bring to a boil, then reduce the heat to medium-low and cook for 15–20 minutes or until all the water has been absorbed and rice is tender.

Meanwhile, smear the chops with the remaining curry paste and marinate for 5 minutes. Heat the remaining oil in a frying pan over high heat, then cook the chops for 3–4 minutes on each side or until cooked to your liking. Remove from the heat, cover with aluminum foil, and allow to rest. Combine the remaining yogurt with 1 tablespoon of the mint.

To serve, stir the remaining mint through the rice, season, then divide among four serving plates. Top with the remaining onions, the lamb, and the almonds. Serve with a dollop of the minted yogurt on the side.

Serves 4

Pan

Rib-eye steak with mixed mushrooms and sherry

4 cups large broccoli florets
1/2 lb. green beans, ends removed
1 tablespoon vegetable oil
1/4 cup butter
4 5-oz. rib-eye steaks, about
 1 in. thick
3 cloves garlic, finely chopped
3 cups mixed mushrooms (portobello,
 shiitake, or button)
2 teaspoons chopped fresh thyme
1/2 cup dry sherry

Bring a saucepan of lightly salted water to a boil. Add the broccoli and beans and cook for 3–4 minutes or until tender but still crisp. Drain.

Melt the oil and 1 tablespoon of the butter in a large stainless-steel frying pan. Cook the steaks for 3–4 minutes on each side for medium-rare or until cooked to your liking. Remove from the pan, cover with aluminum foil, and allow to rest.

Melt another tablespoon of the butter in the saucepan over medium heat. Add the garlic and mushrooms and season. Cook for 3–4 minutes or until the mushrooms have softened. Stir in the thyme. Remove from the pan.

Add the sherry and any juices from the rested meat to the pan and stir to scrape up any sediment from the bottom. Bring to a boil, then reduce the heat and simmer for 2–3 minutes or until reduced to 1/3 cup and thickened slightly. Whisk in the remaining butter in small amounts until glossy.

To serve, put the steaks on four serving plates, top with the mushrooms, and spoon the sauce over the top. Serve with the broccoli and green beans.

Serves 4

Deep-fried calamari in chickpea batter with parsley salad

Deep-fried calamari
1 1/4 cups besan (chickpea flour)
1 1/2 teaspoons bittersweet, smoked
 paprika or regular paprika
1 1/2 teaspoons ground cumin
1/2 teaspoon baking powder
1 cup soda water
vegetable oil, for deep-frying
6 cleaned squid bodies, cut into rings
 about 1/2-in. wide

Parsley salad
1/4 lemon, rinsed, pith and
 flesh removed
1/4 cup lemon juice
1/4 cup extra-virgin olive oil
1 clove garlic, finely chopped
1 cup fresh Italian parsley
harissa, to serve (optional)

To make the batter, sift the besan, paprika, cumin, and baking powder into a bowl, add 1/4 teaspoon pepper, mix together, and make a well in the center. Gradually add the soda water, whisking until smooth. Season with salt. Cover, then leave for 30 minutes.

Cut the lemon rind into very thin slivers. To make the dressing, whisk the lemon juice, extra-virgin olive oil, and garlic together in a bowl.

Fill a large heavy-bottomed saucepan or wok one-third full of oil and heat until a cube of bread dropped into the oil browns in 15 seconds.

Dip the squid into the batter, allowing any excess to drip away. Cook in batches for 30–60 seconds or until pale gold and crisp all over. Drain well on crumpled paper towels and keep warm.

Add the parsley and lemon slivers to the dressing, tossing to coat the leaves. Divide the leaves among four bowls or plates. Top with the calamari rings and serve with harissa.

Serves 4 as an entrée

Sesame-coated tuna with cilantro salsa

4 tuna steaks
¾ cup sesame seeds
3 handfuls baby arugula leaves

Cilantro salsa
1 large clove garlic, crushed
2 tomatoes, seeded and diced
2 tablespoons finely chopped
  fresh cilantro leaves
2 tablespoons virgin olive oil,
  plus extra for frying
1 tablespoon lime juice

Cut each tuna steak into three pieces. Place the sesame seeds on a sheet of baking paper. Roll the tuna in the sesame seeds to coat. Refrigerate for 15 minutes.

To make the salsa, place the garlic, tomatoes, cilantro, oil, and lime juice in a bowl and mix together well. Refrigerate until ready to use.

Fill a heavy-bottomed frying pan to ½ in. with the extra oil and place over high heat. Add the tuna in two batches and cook for 2 minutes each side (it should be pink in the center). Remove and drain on paper towels. To serve, divide the arugula among four serving plates and arrange the tuna over the top. Spoon the salsa on the side and serve immediately.

Serves 4

Veal scaloppine with white wine and parsley

4 5-oz. veal cutlets
1 1/2 tablespoons butter
1/4 cup dry white wine or
  dry Marsala (not sweet)
1/2 cup heavy whipping cream
1 tablespoon whole-grain mustard
2 tablespoons chopped fresh
  Italian parsley

Place the veal cutlets between two sheets of plastic wrap and either press down hard with the heel of your hand until flattened or flatten with a rolling pin or mallet. Heat the butter in a frying pan and cook the cutlets in batches for 1 minute each side or until just cooked. Remove and cover.

Add the wine to the pan, bring to a boil, and cook for 1–2 minutes or until reduced by half. Then add the cream, bring to a boil, and reduce by half again. Stir in the mustard and 1 tablespoon parsley until just combined. Return the veal to the pan to warm through and coat in the sauce. Serve the veal with a little sauce and sprinkle with the remaining parsley. Serve with potatoes and a green salad, if desired.

Serves 4

Salt and pepper chicken with Asian greens and oyster sauce

1¼ cups jasmine rice
⅓ cup all-purpose flour
¾ teaspoon five-spice powder
1½ teaspoons sea salt
1 teaspoon ground white pepper
1½ lbs. boneless chicken breasts,
  cut into thin strips (½ x 2 in.)
½ cup peanut oil
2½ lbs. mixed Asian greens
  (bok choy, choy sum, or gai larn)
½ cup oyster sauce

Bring a large saucepan of water to a boil. Add the rice and cook for 12 minutes, stirring occasionally. Drain well.

Meanwhile, combine the flour, five-spice powder, salt, and pepper in a large bowl. Toss the chicken strips in the flour until well coated. Heat ¼ cup of the oil in a large frying pan over medium-high heat. Add the chicken in three batches and cook, turning, for 3 minutes or until browned. Drain on crumpled paper towels and keep warm.

Heat the remaining oil and cook the mixed Asian greens over medium-high heat for 1–2 minutes. Add the oyster sauce and toss through. Serve on a bed of jasmine rice topped with the chicken strips.

Serves 4

Lamb fillets with spiced lentils and mint raita

½ cup plain yogurt
2 tablespoons finely chopped
  fresh mint
1 tablespoon garam masala
3 teaspoons ground cumin
½ teaspoon chili powder
⅓ cup vegetable oil
4 5-oz lamb fillets
2 teaspoons grated fresh ginger
1 teaspoon ground turmeric
2 14-oz. cans lentils, drained
  and rinsed

Combine the yogurt and half the mint in a small nonmetallic bowl. Cover and set aside.

Dry-fry the garam masala in a frying pan over medium heat for 1 minute or until fragrant. Remove, then dry-fry the cumin. Combine 2 teaspoons each of garam masala and cumin, the chili powder, and 2 tablespoons oil. Put the lamb in a nonmetallic dish. Brush with the spiced oil, cover, and marinate for 10 minutes or overnight.

Meanwhile, heat 1 tablespoon of the remaining oil in a saucepan. Add the ginger, turmeric, and remaining cumin and cook for 30 seconds or until fragrant. Add the lentils and stir until heated through. Reduce the heat to low, add the remaining garam masala, and season with salt. Cover and cook for 5 minutes, adding ¼ cup water if the lentils start to stick. Before serving, stir in the remaining mint.

Heat a large frying pan over medium-high heat and add the remaining oil. Cook the fillets for 3–4 minutes on each side for medium-rare or until cooked to your liking. Leave for several minutes, then cut into ½-in. slices. Place some lentils on a plate, arrange the lamb slices on top, and serve with mint raita.

Serves 4

Swordfish with tomato salsa and garlic mashed potatoes

1 lb. potatoes, cubed
2 large vine-ripened tomatoes
2 tablespoons finely shredded
  fresh basil
1 tablespoon balsamic vinegar
3 cloves garlic, finely chopped
½ cup extra-virgin olive oil
4 7-oz. swordfish steaks

Cook the potatoes in a large saucepan of boiling water for 12–15 minutes or until tender.

To make the salsa, score a cross in the bottom of each tomato. Place in a heatproof bowl and cover with boiling water. Leave for 30 seconds, then plunge into iced water and peel away from the cross. Cut the tomatoes in half, scoop out the seeds, and discard. Finely dice the flesh, then combine with the basil, vinegar, 2 cloves garlic, and 2 tablespoons oil. Season.

Heat ¼ cup of the olive oil in a large nonstick frying pan over medium-high heat. Season the swordfish, then add it to the frying pan and cook for 2–3 minutes on each side for medium-rare or until cooked to your liking.

Just before the swordfish is ready, drain the potatoes. Add the remaining olive oil and garlic and season to taste. Mash until smooth with a potato masher.

To serve, put the swordfish steaks on four serving plates and top with the tomato salsa. Serve the garlic mashed potatoes on the side.

Serves 4

Pork with paprika, potatoes, and shallots

1 tablespoon paprika
4 thick pork loin chops
2 tablespoons extra-virgin olive oil
1/4 cup sherry vinegar
1/4 teaspoon cayenne pepper
1/2 cup puréed tomatoes
13 oz. potatoes, cut into 3/4-in. cubes
8 shallots, peeled
6 handfuls arugula leaves

Combine the paprika with 1/4 teaspoon each of salt and freshly ground black pepper. Sprinkle over both sides of the pork. Heat the oil over medium heat in a deep frying pan large enough to fit the chops in a single layer. Cook the chops until brown on both sides.

Pour the sherry vinegar into the pan and stir well to scrape up any sediment stuck to the bottom. Stir in the cayenne pepper, puréed tomatoes, and 1 cup hot water. Bring to a boil, then add the potatoes and shallots. Reduce the heat, cover, and simmer for 30 minutes or until the sauce has thickened and reduced by half—check the liquid level and add a little water if necessary. Season.

To serve, divide the arugula leaves among four serving plates and place a chop on top. Spoon the sauce and potatoes over the top.

Serves 4

Salt and pepper calamari

1 cup cornstarch
1 1/2 tablespoons salt
1 tablespoon ground white pepper
3 small fresh red chilies,
    seeded and chopped
2 lbs. cleaned squid bodies, sliced
    into rings
2 egg whites, lightly beaten
vegetable oil, for deep-frying
lime wedges, for serving

Combine the cornstarch, salt, pepper, and chilies in a bowl.

Dip the squid rings into the egg white and then into the cornstarch mixture. Shake off any excess cornstarch.

Fill a deep, heavy-bottomed saucepan one third full of oil and heat to 350°F or until a cube of bread dropped into the oil browns in 15 seconds. Cook the squid in batches for 1–2 minutes or until lightly golden all over. Drain on crumpled paper towels. Serve hot with steamed rice and lime wedges.

Serves 4

Japanese-style steak salad

1 1/2 lbs. rump steak
3 teaspoons vegetable oil
3 teaspoons wasabi paste
1/2 teaspoon Dijon mustard
1 teaspoon grated fresh ginger
2 tablespoons rice wine vinegar
3 tablespoons pickled ginger, plus
   1 tablespoon pickling liquid
2 tablespoons sesame oil
1/4 cup vegetable oil, extra
2 cups baby spinach leaves
2 cups mizuna or watercress,
   trimmed
4 radishes, thinly sliced
1 cucumber, peeled and cut into
   ribbons with a vegetable peeler
1/4 cup sesame seeds, toasted

Generously season the steak with salt and freshly cracked black pepper. Heat 3 teaspoons vegetable oil in a large frying pan until very hot. Add the steak and cook for 2–3 minutes on each side or until browned. Remove and allow to rest, covered, for 5 minutes.

Put the wasabi paste, mustard, ginger, rice wine vinegar, pickled ginger, pickling liquid, and 1/2 teaspoon salt in a large bowl and whisk together. Whisk in the oils, then add the spinach, mizuna, radish, and cucumber to the bowl and toss well.

Slice the steak across the grain into thin strips. Divide the salad among four serving plates, top with the beef slices, and sprinkle with sesame seeds. Serve immediately.

Serves 4

Stuffed chicken breast with tomatoes, goat cheese, and asparagus

4 large boneless chicken breasts
2/3 cup sun-dried tomatoes
3 1/2 oz. goat cheese, sliced
12 asparagus spears, trimmed, halved, and blanched
1/4 cup butter
1 1/2 cups chicken stock
2 zucchini, cut into 2-in. sticks
1 cup whipping cream
8 scallions, thinly sliced

Pound each chicken breast between two sheets of plastic wrap with a mallet or rolling pin until 1/2 in. thick. Divide the tomatoes, goat cheese, and 1 1/4 cups of the asparagus pieces among the breasts. Roll up tightly lengthwise, securing along the seam with toothpicks.

Heat the butter in a large frying pan over medium heat. Add the chicken, then brown on all sides. Pour in the stock, then reduce the heat to low. Cook, covered, for 10 minutes or until the chicken is cooked through. Remove the chicken and keep warm.

Meanwhile, bring a saucepan of lightly salted water to a boil. Add the zucchini and remaining asparagus and cook for 2 minutes or until just tender. Remove from the saucepan. Whisk the cream into the frying pan. Add the scallions and simmer over medium-low heat for 4 minutes or until reduced and thickened. To serve, cut each chicken roll in half diagonally and place on a serving plate. Spoon on the sauce and serve with the greens.

Serves 4

Beer-battered fish fillets with chips

¼ cup self-rising flour
¼ cup cornstarch
1 cup all-purpose flour
1 cup beer (any type)
vegetable oil, for deep-frying
4 large, red-skinned, waxy potatoes, cut into french fries
4 6-oz. flathead fillets or other white fish fillets (snapper or John Dory), skin and bones removed
2 lemons, cut into wedges

Preheat the oven to 350°F. Sift the self-rising flour, cornstarch, and ½ cup of the all-purpose flour into a large bowl and make a well. Gradually whisk in the beer to make a smooth batter. Cover.

Fill a large heavy-bottomed saucepan one-third full of oil and heat to 350°F or until a cube of bread dropped into the oil browns in 15 seconds. Deep-fry batches of fries for 2–4 minutes or until pale golden. Drain on paper towels. Deep-fry again for 3 minutes or until golden and cooked through. Keep hot in the oven while you cook the fish.

Reheat the oil to 350°F. Stir the batter, then coat the fish fillets in the remaining all-purpose flour, shaking off the excess. Dip the fillets into the batter, allowing the excess to drip off a little. Slowly ease the fillets into the hot oil, holding the tail out for a few seconds—turn with tongs if necessary. Cook for 4–5 minutes or until golden brown and the fish is cooked through. Remove with a slotted spoon and drain on crumpled paper towels. Serve with the fries, lemon wedges, and a green salad.

Serves 4

Nori omelette with stir-fried vegetables

8 eggs
4 x 7-in. sheet nori
1/4 cup vegetable oil
1 clove garlic, crushed
3 teaspoons finely grated fresh ginger
1 carrot, cut into thick matchsticks
2 zucchini, halved lengthwise and
  sliced diagonally
2 1/4 cups mixed portobello, enoki,
  and oyster mushrooms, sliced
  if large
1 tablespoon Japanese soy sauce
1 tablespoon mirin
2 teaspoons yellow miso paste

Lightly beat the eggs. Roll the nori up tightly and snip with scissors into very fine strips. Add to the eggs and season to taste with salt and cracked black pepper.

Heat a wok over high heat, add 2 teaspoons of the oil, and swirl to coat the side of the wok. Add 1/3 cup of the egg mixture and swirl to coat the bottom of the wok. Cook for 2 minutes or until set, then turn over and cook the other side for 1 minute. Remove and keep warm. Repeat with the remaining mixture, adding another 2 teaspoons of the oil each time, to make four omelettes.

Heat the remaining oil in the wok, add the garlic and ginger, and stir-fry for 1 minute. Add the carrot, zucchini, and mushrooms in two batches and stir-fry for 3 minutes or until softened. Return all the vegetables to the wok. Add the soy sauce, mirin, and miso paste and simmer for 1 minute. Divide the vegetables evenly among the omelettes, roll them up, and serve immediately with steamed rice.

Serves 4

Teriyaki chicken with ginger chive rice

4 5-oz. boneless chicken breasts,
  with skin
1/4 cup Japanese soy sauce
2 tablespoons sake
1 1/2 tablespoons mirin
1 1/2 tablespoons light brown sugar
3 teaspoons finely grated fresh ginger
1 1/2 cups long-grain rice
2 tablespoons finely chopped
  fresh chives
2 tablespoons vegetable oil

Pound each breast between sheets of plastic wrap with a mallet until 1/2 in. thick. Put the soy sauce, sake, mirin, sugar, and 1 teaspoon ginger in a flat, nonmetallic dish and stir until the sugar has dissolved. Add the chicken and turn to coat. Cover and refrigerate for 1 hour, turning once halfway through.

Bring a large saucepan of water to a boil. Add the rice and cook for 12 minutes, stirring occasionally. Drain. Stir in the chives and remaining ginger, then cover until ready to serve.

Drain the chicken, reserving the marinade. Heat the oil in a deep frying pan and cook the chicken, skin-side down, over medium heat for 5 minutes, until the skin is crisp. Turn and cook for another 4 minutes (it won't be totally cooked).

Add the marinade and 1/4 cup water to the pan and scrape up any sediment. Bring to a boil over high heat, then add the chicken (skin-side up) and juices. Cook for 5–6 minutes, until cooked through, turning once. (If the sauce is runny, remove the chicken and boil the sauce until syrupy.) Serve the chicken whole or sliced, drizzled with the sauce.

Serves 4

Salmon and dill potato patties with lime mayonnaise

3/4 lb. new potatoes, cut in half
2 teaspoons grated lime zest
1 1/4 cups mayonnaise
14-oz. can salmon, drained,
  bones removed
1 tablespoon chopped fresh dill
2 scallions, thinly sliced
1 egg
1 cup fresh breadcrumbs
1/4 cup vegetable oil
7 handfuls arugula leaves
lime wedges, to serve

Cook the potatoes in a large saucepan of boiling water for 12–15 minutes or until tender. Drain well and cool.

Meanwhile, combine the lime zest and 1 cup of the mayonnaise.

Transfer the potatoes to a large bowl, then mash roughly with the back of a spoon, leaving some large chunks. Stir in the salmon, dill, and scallions, and season. Mix in the egg and the remaining mayonnaise. Divide into eight portions, forming palm-size patties. Press lightly into the breadcrumbs to coat.

Heat the oil in a nonstick frying pan and cook the patties, turning, for 3–4 minutes or until golden brown. Drain on paper towels. Serve with a dollop of lime mayonnaise, arugula leaves, and lime wedges.

Serves 4

Spice-crusted salmon and noodle salad

1/2 teaspoon wasabi paste
1/3 cup Japanese soy sauce
5 tablespoons mirin
1 teaspoon sugar
1/2 lb. dried somen noodles
1 teaspoon sesame oil
1 teaspoon sansho powder
1 tablespoon vegetable oil
3 6-oz. salmon fillets, skin removed
4 scallions, finely sliced diagonally
1/2 cup cilantro leaves
1 cucumber, halved lengthwise and
  thinly sliced

Combine the wasabi with a little of the Japanese soy sauce to form a smooth paste. Stir in the mirin, sugar, and remaining soy sauce.

Cook the noodles in a large saucepan of boiling salted water for 2 minutes or until tender. Drain and rinse in cold water. Transfer to a large bowl and toss with the sesame oil.

Combine the sansho powder, oil, and 1/4 teaspoon salt and brush on both sides of the salmon. Heat a large frying pan over medium heat. Add the salmon and cook each side for 2–3 minutes or until cooked to your liking. Remove from the saucepan and flake into large pieces with a fork.

Add the salmon, scallions, cilantro, cucumber, and half the dressing to the noodles, then toss together. Place on a serving dish and drizzle with the remaining dressing.

Serves 4

Beef stroganoff

1 1/4 lb. beef rib-eye or rump steaks
1/4 cup seasoned all-purpose flour
3/4 lb. fettuccine or tagliatelle
1/4 cup butter
1 small onion, finely chopped
3 3/4 cups button mushrooms,
   thickly sliced
1 tablespoon tomato paste
1/4 cup red wine
1 1/4 cups whipping cream

Pound the slices of beef between two sheets of plastic wrap with a mallet or rolling pin until they are half their thickness. Cut each slice into strips about 1/2 in. wide. Place in a plastic bag with the seasoned flour and shake to coat the beef.

Cook the pasta in a large saucepan of rapidly boiling salted water until al dente.

Meanwhile, melt 2 tablespoons of the butter in a frying pan over medium heat and cook the onion for 2 minutes. Add the beef in batches and cook for 5 minutes or until evenly browned. Remove from the pan and keep warm. Heat the remaining butter in the pan and add the mushrooms, stirring, for 2–3 minutes or until soft and lightly browned. Add the tomato paste and the red wine, stirring continuously for 2 minutes or until the sauce has reduced. Add the beef, stir in the cream, then reduce the heat to medium-low and simmer gently for another minute or until the sauce has thickened. Serve with the pasta.

Serves 4

Mediterranean burgers

1 large red pepper
1 lb. ground lamb
1 egg, lightly beaten
1 small onion, grated
3 cloves garlic, crushed
2 tablespoons pine nuts, chopped
1 tablespoon finely chopped
  fresh mint
1 tablespoon finely chopped
  fresh Italian parsley
1 teaspoon ground cumin
2 teaspoons chili sauce
1 tablespoon extra-virgin olive oil
4 rolls or pita bread rounds
1 cup store-bought hummus
3 handfuls baby arugula leaves
1 small cucumber, cut into ribbons
chili sauce, to serve (optional)

Cut the pepper into large pieces, removing the seeds and membrane. Place, skin-side up, under the broiler until the skin blackens and blisters. Cool in a plastic bag, then peel and cut into thick strips.

Combine the lamb, egg, onion, garlic, pine nuts, fresh herbs, cumin, and chili sauce in a large bowl. Mix with your hands and roll into four even-size balls. Press the balls into large patties 3½ inches in diameter.

Heat the oil in a large frying pan and cook the patties over medium heat for 6 minutes each side or until well browned and cooked through, then drain on paper towels.

Halve the rolls and toast both sides. Spread the cut sides of the rolls with hummus, then lay arugula leaves, roasted pepper, and cucumber ribbons over the bottom. Place a patty on the salad and top with the other half of the roll. Serve with chili sauce.

Serves 4

Chicken breasts with mustard cream sauce

4 6-oz. chicken breasts
2 tablespoons vegetable oil
1 clove garlic, crushed
1/4 cup dry white wine
2 tablespoons whole-grain mustard
2 teaspoons chopped fresh thyme
1 1/4 cups whipping cream
2 cups green beans, ends removed
3/4 lb. baby yellow squash, halved

Pound each chicken breast between sheets of plastic wrap with a mallet or rolling pin until about 1/2 in. thick.

Heat the oil in a frying pan over high heat. Brown the chicken breasts for 4–5 minutes on each side or until brown. Remove and cover with aluminum foil.

Add the garlic to the frying pan and cook for 1 minute over medium heat, then stir in the wine, mustard, and thyme. Increase the heat to medium-high and pour in the cream. Simmer for 5 minutes or until the sauce has reduced and thickened slightly, then season to taste.

Meanwhile, bring a saucepan of lightly salted water to a boil, add the beans and squash, and cook for 2–4 minutes or until just tender. Season to taste. To serve, pour a little of the sauce over the chicken and serve with the vegetables on the side.

Serves 4

Fish fillets with fennel and red pepper salsa

1 ½ lbs. small new potatoes
1 teaspoon fennel seeds
½ cup extra-virgin olive oil
2 tablespoons drained baby capers
1 small red pepper, seeded and finely
  diced
8 handfuls mixed lettuce leaves,
  washed
2 tablespoons balsamic vinegar
4 6-oz. white fish fillets (John Dory or
  other firm white fish)

Cook the potatoes in a saucepan of boiling water for 15–20 minutes or until tender. Drain and keep warm.

Meanwhile, to make the salsa, dry-fry the fennel seeds in a frying pan over medium heat for 1 minute or until fragrant. Remove the seeds and heat 1 tablespoon of oil in the same pan over medium heat. When the oil is hot but not smoking, flash-fry the capers for 1–2 minutes or until crisp. Remove from the pan. Heat 1 tablespoon oil and cook the pepper, stirring, for 4–5 minutes or until cooked through. Remove and combine with the fennel seeds and fried capers.

Place the lettuce leaves in a serving bowl. To make the dressing, combine the balsamic vinegar and ¼ cup of the olive oil in a bowl. Add 1 tablespoon to the salsa, then toss the rest through the lettuce leaves.

Wipe the frying pan, then heat the remaining oil over medium-high heat. Season the fish well. When the oil is hot but not smoking, cook the fish for 2–3 minutes each side or until cooked through. Serve immediately with the salsa, potatoes, and salad.

Serves 4

Rare fillet of beef with cellophane noodles and ginger dressing

3/4-lb. fillet of beef
2 tablespoons peanut oil
1/2 lb. cellophane noodles
1/2 teaspoon sesame oil
2 scallions, thinly sliced diagonally

Ginger dressing
1 1/2 tablespoons finely chopped
  fresh ginger
3 tablespoons light soy sauce
3 tablespoons mirin
1 teaspoon sugar
2 teaspoons rice wine vinegar

Trim the beef of excess fat and sinew, then season with ground black pepper. Heat the peanut oil in a large frying pan. When very hot, sear the meat in batches on all sides for 3 minutes or until brown. The meat needs to remain very pink on the inside. Remove from the frying pan and allow to cool. Cover and refrigerate until completely cold.

Place the noodles in a heatproof bowl, cover with boiling water, and soak for 3–4 minutes. Drain and rinse under cold water. Return the noodles to the bowl, add the sesame oil, and toss well together.

To make the ginger dressing, combine the chopped ginger in a small bowl with the light soy sauce, mirin, sugar, and rice wine vinegar, stirring until the sugar has completely dissolved. Set aside until ready to use.

Add half the scallion slices to the bowl of noodles, toss together well, then place on a large serving platter. Cut the beef into thin slices, then arrange in a mound on top of the noodles.

Warm the dressing slightly over low heat, then pour over the beef and noodles. Sprinkle over the remaining scallion slices and serve immediately.

Serves 4

Pork chops with apple and red onion chutney

1/2 cup butter
2 small red onions, sliced
2 Granny Smith apples, peeled, cored, then cut into quarters and sliced
1/4 teaspoon ground cloves
1/3 cup honey
4 8-oz. pork loin chops
2 teaspoons vegetable oil
1 tablespoon butter, extra
1/2 teaspoon caraway seeds
1 1/2 lbs. green cabbage, thinly shredded

To make the chutney, melt 1/4 cup of the butter in a saucepan, then add the onions, apples, cloves, and honey. Simmer, covered, for 10 minutes over low heat. Increase the heat to medium, cover, and cook for another 20 minutes or until the liquid is reduced to a thick chutney. Allow to cool.

Meanwhile, season the chops well on both sides with salt and ground black pepper. Heat the oil and 1/4 cup of the butter in a large frying pan and sauté the chops over medium-high heat for 6–8 minutes on each side or until browned and cooked through. Remove the pan from the heat and allow the chops to rest for 2 minutes.

While the chops are cooking, melt the extra butter in a large saucepan, add the caraway seeds and cabbage, and cook, covered, over medium-low heat, tossing a few times with tongs, for 12 minutes or until tender.

To serve, place a pork chop on each plate and serve the cabbage on the side. Top with a spoonful of chutney.

Serves 4

Pan-fried lamb fillets with red wine

1 1/4 lbs. small new potatoes
1 1/2 cups snow peas, trimmed
2 tablespoons extra-virgin olive oil
4 6-oz. lamb fillets, trimmed
2/3 cup red wine
1 tablespoon grape jelly
2 teaspoons chopped fresh thyme
1 1/2 tablespoons butter, chilled and
   cut into cubes

Cook the potatoes in a large saucepan of lightly salted boiling water for 15–20 minutes or until tender. Add the snow peas and cook for another minute. Drain the vegetables, return to the saucepan, and toss gently with 1 tablespoon of the oil.

Meanwhile, heat the remaining oil in a large frying pan and cook the lamb fillets over medium-high heat for 4–5 minutes on each side or until cooked but still pink inside. Remove from the saucepan, cover, and keep warm.

Add the wine, jelly, and thyme to the saucepan and bring to a boil. Boil rapidly for 5 minutes or until reduced and syrupy. Stir in the butter. To serve, slice the lamb diagonally, divide among four plates, and spoon some sauce on top. Serve with the vegetables.

Serves 4

Sweet chili and ginger swordfish

4 swordfish steaks
1/4 cup peanut oil
3 cloves garlic, finely chopped
2 tablespoons grated fresh ginger
1/4 cup lime juice
1/3 cup sweet chili sauce

Place the swordfish steaks in a nonmetallic bowl, brush lightly with a little of the oil, and top each steak with some mixed garlic and ginger.

Heat the remaining oil in a nonstick frying pan. Add the swordfish with the topping facing up. Cook over medium heat for 2 minutes or until crisp and golden on the underside.

Combine 1 tablespoon each of the lime juice and sweet chili sauce and drizzle over the steaks. Carefully turn over and cook for 2 minutes or until tender but still pink in the middle. Remove and keep warm.

Add the remaining lime juice and sweet chili sauce, bring to a boil, and cook for 1 minute or until the sauce is thickened. Serve with steamed rice and stir-fried vegetables.

Serves 4

Sausages and mashed potatoes with shallot gravy

1/3 cup extra-virgin olive oil
6 oz. shallots, thinly sliced
1 tablespoon all-purpose flour
1/2 cup red wine
1 1/2 cups beef stock
1 tablespoon Dijon mustard
3 lbs. potatoes, chopped
2/3 cup butter
8 4-oz. pork sausages
1 lb. green beans, ends removed

Heat 2 tablespoons oil in a large frying pan over medium heat. Add the shallots and cook for 5 minutes, stirring often until they soften. Add the flour and cook for 30 seconds. Increase the heat, pour in the wine and stock, and bring to a boil. Reduce the heat and simmer for 10 minutes or until the gravy thickens. Stir in the mustard, then reduce the heat to medium-low and simmer gently until the sausages and mashed potatoes are ready.

Cook the potatoes in boiling water until tender. Drain, return to the pan, and add 1 tablespoon olive oil and 1/2 cup butter. Mash until smooth, then season with salt and pepper.

While the potatoes are cooking, prick the sausages with a fork. Heat a large frying pan over medium-high heat and add the remaining oil and the sausages. Cook for 10 minutes or until cooked through, turning often.

Bring a saucepan of lightly salted water to a boil, add the beans, and cook for 4 minutes or until just tender. Whisk the remaining butter into the gravy and season. Serve the sausages on the mashed potatoes, with green beans on the side.

Serves 4

Spanish saffron chicken and rice

¼ cup extra-virgin olive oil
4 chicken thighs and 6 drumsticks
1 large red onion, finely chopped
1 large green pepper, two thirds diced
  and one third julienned
3 teaspoons sweet paprika
14-oz. can diced tomatoes
1¼ cups paella or arborio rice
½ teaspoon ground saffron

Heat 2 tablespoons of the oil in a large, deep frying pan over high heat. Season the chicken pieces well and brown in batches. Remove the chicken from the pan.

Reduce to medium heat and add the remaining oil to the pan. Add the onion and the diced pepper and cook gently for 5 minutes. Stir in the paprika and cook for 30 seconds. Add the tomatoes and simmer for 1–3 minutes or until it thickens.

Stir 3½ cups boiling water into the pan, then add the rice and saffron. Return the chicken to the pan and stir to combine. Season. Bring to a boil, then cover, reduce the heat to medium-low, and simmer for 20–30 minutes or until all the liquid has been absorbed and the chicken is tender. Stir in the julienned pepper, then allow to rest, covered, for 3–4 minutes before serving.

Serves 4

Classic omelette

12 eggs
2 tablespoons butter

Break the eggs into a bowl. Add
$1/2$ cup water, season with salt and
freshly ground black pepper, and beat
together well. Heat 2 teaspoons of
the butter in a small frying pan over
high heat. When the butter is foaming,
reduce the heat to medium and add a
quarter of the egg mixture. Tilt the
pan to cover the base with the egg
and leave for a few seconds. Using a
spatula, draw the sides of the
omelette into the center and let any
extra liquid egg run to the edges.

If you are adding a filling to the
omelette, sprinkle it over the egg. As
soon as the egg is almost set, use a
spatula or egg slide to fold the
omelette in half in the pan. It should
still be soft inside. Slide it onto a
warm serving plate and repeat to
make three more omelettes.

Serves 4

Fillings: Sprinkle each omelette with
$1/3$ cup roughly torn arugula leaves
and 2 oz. crumbled goat cheese.
    Or, sauté 3 cups finely sliced button
mushrooms with $1/4$ cup butter, add
4 tablespoons finely chopped fresh
basil, and use some of the mixture for
sprinkling over each omelette.

Veal scaloppine with sage

1 1/4 lbs. small new potatoes, halved
1/3 cup extra-virgin olive oil
8 small veal scaloppine slices or
  schnitzels
4 slices pancetta, cut in half
  lengthwise
8 fresh sage leaves
1 cup marsala
15 asparagus spears

Preheat the oven to 400°F. Boil the potatoes for 10 minutes. Drain and transfer to a baking sheet with 2 tablespoons olive oil. Toss well and bake for 40–50 minutes or until crisp.

Pound each veal slice between sheets of plastic wrap with a mallet until 1/4 in. thick. Press a piece of pancetta and a sage leaf onto each slice, then skewer with a toothpick. Season to taste.

Heat the remaining oil in a large heavy-bottomed frying pan. Place the scaloppine pancetta-side down in the pan (do in batches if necessary) and cook for 1–2 minutes. Turn and cook for 1 minute. Remove from the pan and keep warm. Add the marsala and cook for 4–5 minutes or until syrupy and reduced by half. Return the scaloppine to the pan and toss lightly in the sauce until warmed through.

When the potatoes are nearly ready, bring a large saucepan of lightly salted water to a boil and cook the asparagus for 3 minutes. Drain.

Remove the toothpicks and divide the scaloppine among serving plates. Drizzle any pan juices on top. Serve with the asparagus and potatoes.

Serves 4

Tuna steaks with olive mayonnaise and potato wedges

3 large, red-skinned, waxy potatoes,
   unpeeled and cut lengthwise
   into 8 wedges
1 1/3 cups extra-virgin olive oil
2 egg yolks, at room temperature
1 tablespoon lemon juice
1/3 cup pitted black olives,
   finely chopped
7 handfuls baby arugula leaves
1 tablespoon finely chopped
   fresh rosemary
4 6-oz. tuna steaks

Preheat the oven to 400°F. Toss the potatoes with 2 tablespoons oil in a baking pan. Bake for 45–50 minutes or until crisp and golden.

Meanwhile, process the egg yolks in a food processor, adding 1/4 cup of the oil drop by drop. With the motor running, pour in 3/4 cup of the oil in a thin stream until the mixture thickens and becomes creamy. With the motor still running, add 1 teaspoon of the lemon juice, season with salt, and blend for 30 seconds. Stir in the olives, cover, and refrigerate.

To make the salad, toss the arugula leaves, 2 tablespoons oil, and 1 tablespoon lemon juice in a bowl.

Press the rosemary into the tuna steaks. Heat the remaining tablespoon of oil in a large frying pan and sear the tuna steaks over medium-high heat for 2–3 minutes on each side or until cooked to your liking. Serve with a dollop of olive mayonnaise, potato wedges, and arugula salad.

Serves 4

Note: To save time, substitute 1 cup of store-bought mayonnaise.

Parmesan chicken with quick salsa verde

3 eggs
1 cup loosely packed fresh basil
2 tablespoons capers, rinsed
1 tablespoon Dijon mustard
2 tablespoons freshly grated
   Parmesan
3/4 cup extra-virgin olive oil
1 cup dry breadcrumbs
4 4-oz. boneless chicken breasts
5 handfuls arugula leaves
lemon wedges, to serve

Place 1 egg in a saucepan of cold water, bring to a boil, and cook for 1 minute. Remove from the heat and rinse with cold water. Peel, then place in a food processor with the basil, capers, mustard, and 1 tablespoon of the Parmesan until combined. Gradually add 1/4 cup of the olive oil and process until you have a coarse sauce, taking care not to overprocess.

Beat the remaining eggs together with 1 tablespoon water. Combine the breadcrumbs with the remaining Parmesan on a plate. Pound each chicken breast between two sheets of plastic wrap with a mallet or rolling pin until 1/4 in. thick. Dip the chicken in the egg mixture, then coat in the breadcrumb mixture. Place on a paper-lined baking tray and refrigerate for 10 minutes or until needed.

Heat the remaining oil in a large frying pan over high heat. Cook the chicken breasts in batches for 2–3 minutes each batch or until golden on both sides and cooked through—keep each batch warm. Serve with the salsa verde, arugula leaves, and lemon wedges.

Serves 4

Fillet steak with pink peppercorn sauce

¼ cup butter
1 tablespoon vegetable oil
4 New York strip steaks or rump
  steaks
½ cup white wine
2 tablespoons brandy
½ cup beef stock
2 tablespoons pink peppercorns
  in brine, drained and rinsed
½ cup whipping cream

Heat the butter and oil in a large frying pan and cook the steaks over high heat for 3–4 minutes each side or until cooked to your liking. Remove from the pan, cover, and keep warm.

Add the wine and brandy to the pan and simmer for 4 minutes or until reduced by half. Add the beef stock and reduce by half again (you should have just over ½ cup sauce). Meanwhile, roughly chop half the peppercorns.

Stir in all the peppercorns and the cream and cook gently until the sauce has thickened slightly. Place the steaks on four warmed serving plates and spoon the sauce over the top. Serve with a green salad.

Serves 4

Veal schnitzel with dill potato salad

1 1/2 lbs. pink-skinned potatoes, unpeeled
1 lb. veal leg steaks
1/2 cup seasoned all-purpose flour
2 eggs, lightly beaten
1 cup dry breadcrumbs
1/2 cup extra-virgin olive oil
2 tablespoons lemon juice
1 1/2 tablespoons finely chopped fresh dill
7 handfuls mixed lettuce leaves

Cook the potatoes in a large saucepan of boiling water for 15–20 minutes or until tender. Drain, then cut into quarters lengthwise and cover to keep warm.

Meanwhile, beat the veal between two sheets of plastic wrap to 1/4-in. thickness. Coat the veal in the flour, shaking off the excess. Dip the veal in the egg, then coat in breadcrumbs. Place the veal schnitzel on a flat tray, cover, and freeze for 5 minutes.

Heat 1/4 cup of the oil in a large frying pan and cook the veal in two batches over medium-high heat for 2–3 minutes on each side or until golden and cooked through. Drain on crumpled paper towels and keep warm.

Whisk the lemon juice, dill, and remaining oil together in a small bowl and pour over the potatoes. Season with salt and freshly ground black pepper and toss gently. Serve the schnitzel with the potatoes and a mixed salad.

Serves 4

Seared salmon with sesame and cucumber noodles

1/2 lb. buckwheat (soba) noodles
1 1/2 tablespoons sesame oil
2 tablespoons kecap manis (sweet soy sauce)
1 tablespoon Chinese black vinegar
2 cucumbers, julienned
6 scallions, trimmed and sliced diagonally into 1 1/2-in. pieces
2 tablespoons black sesame seeds
1 1/4 lbs. salmon fillet pieces, skin and bones removed

Cook the noodles in a large saucepan of boiling water until tender—this should take 5 minutes. Drain well. Place in a large bowl and mix in 2 teaspoons of the sesame oil, then set aside to cool. Combine the kecap manis, vinegar, and the remaining sesame oil, then toss 1 tablespoon of the mixture through the noodles. Cover the noodles and refrigerate for 2 hours.

Remove the noodles from the refrigerator 20 minutes before serving. Gently mix the noodles, cucumber, scallions, and black sesame seeds.

Heat a large frying pan over medium-high heat. Brush the salmon pieces lightly with oil, and season with salt and freshly ground black pepper. Cook for 1–2 minutes on each side or until cooked to your liking. Remove from the heat and set aside until cool enough to handle. Flake the fish into large pieces and gently incorporate it into the noodles, along with the rest of the dressing—be careful not to overhandle or the salmon will flake into small pieces. Serve immediately.

Serves 4

Note: These noodles need to be marinated for 2 hours, but the rest of the preparation is very quick.

Eggplant, tomato, and goat cheese stacks

1/2 cup extra-virgin olive oil
2 large cloves garlic, crushed
2 small eggplants
2 ripe tomatoes
5 oz. goat cheese
8 basil leaves
small arugula leaves, to garnish

Dressing
1 3/4 cups sun-dried tomatoes,
   drained, reserving 1 tablespoon oil
1 clove garlic, crushed
2 tablespoons white wine vinegar
2 tablespoons mayonnaise

Place the oil and garlic in a bowl and mix together. Cut each eggplant into six 1/2-in. slices, then cut each tomato into four 1/2-in. slices. Using a sharp knife dipped in hot water, cut the cheese into eight 1/2-in. slices.

Brush both sides of the eggplant with half of the oil mixture. Heat a frying pan and cook the eggplant in batches over high heat for 3–4 minutes each side or until golden. Remove and keep warm. Brush both sides of the tomatoes with the remaining oil mixture and cook for 1 minute each side or until sealed and warmed through.

To make the dressing, blend the sun-dried tomatoes, reserved oil, and the garlic in a food processor until smooth. Add the vinegar and process until combined. Transfer to a bowl and stir in the mayonnaise. Season.

To assemble, place an eggplant slice on each plate. Top with a slice of tomato, then a basil leaf and a slice of cheese. Repeat with the remaining ingredients to give two layers, then finish with a third piece of eggplant. Add a dollop of dressing and arrange the arugula around each stack. Serve immediately.

Serves 4

Lemon pepper tuna burger

2 6-oz. cans tuna, drained
juice of 1/2 lemon
1 teaspoon cracked black pepper
1 large onion, chopped
2/3 cup dry breadcrumbs
1 egg, lightly beaten
2 tablespoons chopped fresh
   lemon thyme
1 tablespoon chopped fresh
   Italian parsley
2 teaspoons grated lemon zest
2 tablespoons vegetable oil
1 loaf Turkish bread
1/3 cup mayonnaise
5 handfuls arugula leaves
4 slices cheddar cheese
2 tomatoes, sliced
1 cucumber, sliced
1/2 red onion, sliced

Mix the tuna, lemon juice, black pepper, onion, breadcrumbs, egg, thyme, parsley, and lemon zest in a bowl. Form into four even-sized patties and flatten slightly. Heat a nonstick frying pan with the oil. Cook the patties over medium heat on both sides for 5 minutes or until browned.

Cut the bread into four portions. Cut each portion in half horizontally and place under a broiler to lightly brown.

Spread both cut sides of the bread with mayonnaise. Top with some arugula, and layer with a patty and slices of cheese, tomato, cucumber, and onion. Place the other half of the Turkish bread on top, cut in half, and serve.

Serves 4

Crab, Camembert, and fusilli frittata

1 cup tricolored fusilli
1 tablespoon extra-virgin olive oil
1 very small red onion, finely chopped
1 large Roma tomato, roughly chopped
1/3 cup sun-dried tomatoes, roughly chopped
2 tablespoons finely chopped cilantro leaves
2/3 cup fresh or canned crabmeat, cooked
5 oz. Camembert, rind removed, cut into small pieces
6 eggs plus 2 egg yolks

Cook the pasta in a large saucepan of rapidly boiling salted water until al dente. Drain, rinse, then drain again and set aside to cool. Meanwhile, heat half the oil in a small frying pan over low heat, add the onion, and cook for 4–5 minutes or until softened but not browned. Transfer to a bowl and add the Roma tomato, sun-dried tomatoes, and cilantro. Squeeze out any excess moisture from the crabmeat and add the meat to the bowl. Add half the cheese to the bowl, then add the cooled pasta. Mix well. Beat together the six eggs and the two extra yolks, then stir into the tomato and crab mixture. Season.

Heat the remaining oil in the frying pan, pour in the frittata mixture, and cook over low heat for 25 minutes. Preheat the broiler to low. Sprinkle the remaining Camembert over the frittata before placing it under the broiler for 10–15 minutes or until cooked and golden brown on top. Remove from the broiler and leave for 5 minutes. Cut into slices and serve with salad and fresh bread.

Serves 4–6

Note: Although this recipe can be prepared very quickly, it does take a while to cook.

Orange sweet potato and ditalini patties

2 orange sweet potatoes
   (about 1¾ lbs. total)
½ cup ditalini pasta
¼ cup toasted pine nuts
2 cloves garlic, crushed
4 tablespoons finely chopped
   fresh basil
½ cup grated Parmesan
⅓ cup dry breadcrumbs
all-purpose flour, for dusting
extra-virgin olive oil, for frying

Preheat the oven to 500°F. Pierce the whole orange sweet potatoes several times with a fork, then place in a roasting pan and roast for 1 hour or until soft. Remove and allow to cool. Meanwhile, cook the pasta in a large saucepan of rapidly boiling salted water until al dente. Drain and rinse under running water.

Peel the sweet potatoes and mash the flesh with a potato masher or fork, then add the pine nuts, garlic, basil, Parmesan, breadcrumbs, and the pasta, and combine. Season.

Shape the mixture into eight ½-in.-thick patties with floured hands, then lightly dust the patties with flour. Heat the oil in a large frying pan and cook the patties in batches over medium heat for 2 minutes each side or until golden and heated through. Drain on crumpled paper towels, sprinkle with salt, and serve immediately. Great with a fresh green salad.

Serves 4

Note: Roasting the sweet potatoes is the most time-consuming part of this recipe, and you don't need to be in the kitchen the whole time they are cooking. The rest is easy.

Wok

Beef and bamboo shoots

¼ cup vegetable oil
13-oz. rump steak, thinly sliced
    across the grain
1 cup sliced bamboo shoots, drained
    and rinsed
3 cloves garlic, crushed
¼ teaspoon salt
2 tablespoons fish sauce
8 scallions, cut into 1½-in. pieces
    diagonally
¼ cup sesame seeds, toasted

Heat a wok over high heat, add
2 tablespoons of the oil, and swirl.
When the oil is hot, add the beef in
two batches and stir-fry for 1 minute
or until it starts to turn pink. Remove
and set aside.

Add an extra tablespoon of oil if
necessary, then stir-fry the bamboo
shoots for 3 minutes or until starting
to brown. Add the garlic, fish sauce,
and salt and stir-fry for 2–3 minutes.
Add the scallions and stir-fry for 1
minute or until starting to wilt. Return
the beef to the wok, stir quickly, and
cook for 1 minute until heated
through. Remove from the heat, toss
with the sesame seeds, and serve
with rice.

Serves 4

Orange sweet potato, spinach, and water chestnut stir-fry

1 lb. orange sweet potatoes
1 tablespoon vegetable oil
2 cloves garlic, crushed
2 teaspoons sambal oelek
7-oz. can water chestnuts, sliced
2 teaspoons grated palm sugar
  (see Note)
3/4 lb. spinach, stems removed
2 tablespoons soy sauce
2 tablespoons vegetable stock

Cut the orange sweet potatoes into 1/2-in. cubes. Cook the sweet potatoes in a large saucepan of boiling water for 15 minutes or until tender. Drain well.

Heat a wok until very hot, add the oil, and swirl to coat. Stir-fry the garlic and sambal oelek for 1 minute or until fragrant. Add the sweet potatoes and water chestnuts and stir-fry over medium-high heat for 2 minutes. Reduce the heat to medium, add the sugar, and cook for another 2 minutes or until the sugar has melted. Add the spinach, soy sauce, and stock and toss until the spinach has just wilted. Serve with rice.

Serves 4

Note: Sambal oelek is made from mashed, fresh red chilies, mixed with salt and vinegar or tamarind. Palm sugar is available from Asian markets. Use brown sugar if not available.

Shrimp with spicy tamarind sauce

½ cup cashew nuts
1¼ cups jasmine rice
2 garlic cloves, finely chopped
1½ tablespoons fish sauce
1 tablespoon sambal oelek
1 tablespoon peanut oil
2 lbs. medium shrimp, peeled and deveined, with tails intact
2 teaspoons tamarind concentrate
1½ tablespoons grated palm sugar or brown sugar
¾ lb. choy sum, cut into 4-in. pieces

Preheat the oven to 350°F. Spread the cashews on a baking sheet and bake for 5–8 minutes or until light golden—watch carefully, as they burn easily.

Meanwhile, bring a large saucepan of water to a boil. Add the rice and cook for 12 minutes, stirring occasionally. Drain well.

Place the garlic, fish sauce, sambal oelek, and toasted cashews in a blender or food processor, adding 2–3 tablespoons of water, if needed. Blend to a rough paste.

Heat a wok until very hot, add the oil, and swirl to coat. Add the shrimp and toss for 1–2 minutes or until starting to turn pink. Remove from the wok. Add the cashew paste and stir-fry for 1 minute or until it starts to brown slightly. Add the tamarind, sugar, and ⅓ cup water, then bring to a boil, stirring well. Return the shrimp to the wok and stir to coat. Cook for 2–3 minutes or until the shrimp are cooked through.

Place the choy sum in a paper-lined bamboo steamer and steam over a wok or saucepan of simmering water for 3 minutes or until tender. Serve with the shrimp and rice.

Serves 4

Stir-fried hoisin pork and greens with ginger rice

1 1/4 cups jasmine rice
1 lb. pork fillets, thinly sliced
1 tablespoon sugar
2 tablespoons vegetable oil
1/2 cup white wine vinegar
1 cup hoisin sauce
2 tablespoons stem ginger in syrup, chopped
2 1/4 lbs. mixed Asian greens (bok choy, choy sum, or spinach)

Rinse the rice and place in a large saucepan. Add 1 3/4 cups water and bring to a boil. Cover, reduce the heat to very low, and cook for 10 minutes. Remove from the heat and allow to rest, covered, for 10 minutes.

Meanwhile, place the pork in a bowl and sprinkle with the sugar. Toss to coat. Heat a wok over high heat, add 1 tablespoon oil, and swirl to coat. Add the pork in batches and stir-fry for 3 minutes or until brown. Remove. Add the vinegar to the wok and boil for 3–5 minutes or until reduced by two-thirds. Reduce the heat, add the hoisin sauce and 1 tablespoon ginger, and simmer for 5 minutes. Season to taste. Remove from the wok.

Reheat the cleaned wok over high heat, add the remaining oil, and swirl to coat. Add the greens and stir-fry for 3 minutes or until crisp and cooked. Stir the remaining ginger through the rice, then press into four round teacups or small bowls, smoothing the surface. Unmold the rice onto four serving plates, arrange the pork and greens on the side, and drizzle the sauce over the top.

Serves 4

Beef and Hokkien noodle stir-fry

3/4-lb. fillet of beef, partially frozen
1 cup snow peas
1 1/4 lbs. fresh Hokkien noodles
1 tablespoon peanut oil
1 large onion, cut into thin wedges
1 large carrot, thinly sliced, diagonally
1 medium red pepper, cut into thin
  strips
2 cloves garlic, crushed
1 teaspoon grated fresh ginger
2 1/4 cups fresh shiitake mushrooms,
  sliced
1/4 cup oyster sauce
2 tablespoons light soy sauce
1 tablespoon light brown sugar
1/2 teaspoon five-spice powder

Cut the steak into thin slices. Trim both ends of the snow peas and slice in half diagonally. Soak the noodles in a large bowl with enough boiling water to cover for 10 minutes.

Spray a large wok with oil spray, and when very hot, cook the steak in batches until brown. Remove and keep warm.

Heat the peanut oil in the wok, and when very hot, stir-fry the onion, carrot, and pepper for 2–3 minutes or until tender. Add the garlic, ginger, snow peas, and shiitake mushrooms, and cook for another minute before returning the steak to the wok.

Separate the noodles with a fork, then drain. Add to the wok, tossing well. Combine the oyster sauce with the soy sauce, brown sugar, five-spice powder, and 1 tablespoon water, and pour over the noodles. Toss until warmed through, then serve.

Serves 4

Calamari in black bean and chili sauce

4 squid bodies
2 tablespoons vegetable oil
1 onion, cut into 8 wedges
1 red pepper, sliced
1/4 lb. baby corn, cut in halves
3 scallions, cut into
   1 1/4-in. pieces (optional)

Black bean sauce
3 teaspoons cornstarch
2 tablespoons canned, salted black
   beans, washed and drained
2 small red chilies, seeded
   and chopped
2 cloves garlic, finely chopped
2 teaspoons grated fresh ginger
2 tablespoons oyster sauce
2 teaspoons soy sauce
1 teaspoon sugar

Open out each squid body. Score a shallow diamond pattern over the inside surface of each without cutting through, then cut into 2-in. squares.

For the sauce, mix the cornstarch with 1/2 cup water in a bowl. Place the black beans in a bowl and mash with a fork. Add the chilies, garlic, ginger, oyster and soy sauces, sugar, and the cornstarch mix, and stir.

Heat the oil in a wok and stir the onion for 1 minute over high heat. Add the pepper and corn and stir for another 2 minutes.

Add the squid to the wok and stir for 1–2 minutes, until the flesh curls up. Add the sauce and bring to a boil, stirring constantly, until the sauce thickens. Stir in the scallions. Serve with steamed rice noodles.

Serves 4

Note: Instead of squid, you can use other fish, cuttlefish, shrimp, octopus, or a combination.

Chicken with Thai basil

3 tablespoons peanut oil
1 lb. boneless chicken breasts,
  trimmed and cut into thin strips
1 clove garlic, crushed
4 scallions, thinly sliced
1 1/4 cups snake beans, trimmed
  and cut into 2-in. pieces
2 small, fresh red chilies, thinly sliced
3/4 cup tightly packed, fresh Thai basil
2 tablespoons chopped fresh mint
1 tablespoon fish sauce
1 tablespoon oyster sauce
2 teaspoons lime juice
1 tablespoon grated palm sugar or
  brown sugar
fresh Thai basil, extra, to garnish

Heat a wok over high heat, add
1 tablespoon of the oil, and swirl to
coat. Cook the chicken in batches for
3–5 minutes or until lightly browned
and almost cooked—add more oil if
needed. Remove and keep warm.

Heat the remaining oil. Add the
garlic, onions, snake beans, and
chilies and stir-fry for 1 minute or
until the onions are tender. Add the
chicken to the wok.

Toss in the basil and mint, then add
the combined fish sauce, oyster
sauce, lime juice, sugar, and
2 tablespoons water and cook for
1 minute. Garnish with the extra basil
and serve with jasmine rice.

Serves 4

Red roast duck curry

1 tablespoon peanut oil
2 cloves garlic, crushed
8 scallions, cut into 1¼-in. pieces
1 tablespoon red curry paste,
  or to taste
1²/₃ cups coconut milk
1½ lbs. Chinese roast duck, chopped
1-lb. can pineapple pieces in syrup,
  drained
3 fresh kaffir lime leaves
¼ cup chopped cilantro leaves
2 tablespoons chopped fresh mint

Heat a wok until very hot, add the oil, and swirl to coat. Add the garlic, scallions, and red curry paste, and stir-fry for 1 minute or until fragrant.

Stir in the coconut milk, duck, pineapple, lime leaves, cilantro leaves, and mint. Bring to a boil, then reduce the heat and simmer for 10 minutes or until the duck is heated through. Serve with jasmine rice.

Serves 4–6

Lamb, mint, and chili stir-fry

1¼ cups jasmine rice
2 tablespoons vegetable oil
1½ lbs. lamb fillets, sliced thinly
2 cloves garlic, finely chopped
1 small red onion, cut into wedges
1 fresh bird's eye chili, finely chopped
¼ cup lime juice
2 tablespoons sweet chili sauce
2 tablespoons fish sauce
½ cup fresh mint leaves

Bring a large saucepan of water to a boil. Add the rice and cook for 12 minutes, stirring occasionally. Drain well.

Meanwhile, heat a wok until very hot, add 1 tablespoon oil, and swirl to coat. Add the lamb in batches and cook for 2 minutes or until browned. Remove from the wok.

Heat the remaining oil in the wok, add the garlic and onion, and stir-fry for 1 minute. Add the chili and cook for 30 seconds. Return the lamb to the wok, then add the lime juice, sweet chili sauce, and fish sauce, and stir-fry for 2 minutes over high heat. Stir in the mint and serve with the rice.

Serves 4

Note: You can use chicken breasts or pork loin, adding ½ cup cashews and using basil instead of mint.

Fried rice with Chinese barbecue pork

6 scallions
1 1/2 cups snow peas
6 oz. Chinese barbecue pork
3 teaspoons sesame oil
2 eggs, lightly beaten
2 cloves garlic, finely chopped
3 cups cold, cooked, white long-grain
    rice (see Note)
2 tablespoons soy sauce

Cut the scallions and snow peas diagonally into very thin shreds. Cut the pork into thin slices.

Heat a wok until hot, add 1 teaspoon of the oil, and swirl to coat the bottom. Add the eggs and swirl over the bottom of the wok until just set. Turn over and cook for 30 seconds or until just lightly browned, then remove from the wok. Allow the cooked egg to cool slightly, then roll up and cut into 1/2-in. slices.

While the wok is still very hot, add the remaining oil, then the garlic, scallions, and snow peas. Stir-fry for 1–2 minutes or until slightly soft. Add the pork, rice, soy sauce, and strips of omelette and toss until heated through and thoroughly combined— the soy sauce should turn the rice brown. Remove from the heat and serve immediately.

Serves 4

Note: Cook 1 cup long-grain rice in a large saucepan of boiling water. To cool, spread the rice on a shallow tray and leave uncovered in the refrigerator overnight.

Chili snake beans and noodles

3/4 lb. fresh, flat egg noodles
   (1/4 in. wide)
5 cloves garlic, peeled
3 red Asian shallots, chopped
1 small fresh red chili, seeded
   and chopped
3 fresh cilantro roots, chopped
2 1/2 tablespoons peanut oil
1 lb. snake beans, cut into
   1 1/2-in. pieces
2 1/2 tablespoons fish sauce
1 1/2 tablespoons grated palm
   sugar or brown sugar
1 tablespoon kecap manis
1 tablespoon lime juice
1 tablespoon crisp, fried
   onion flakes
fresh red chili, sliced, to garnish
lime wedges, to garnish

Cook the noodles in a saucepan of boiling water for 1 minute or until tender. Drain well.

Place the garlic, red Asian shallots, chili, and cilantro roots in a mortar and pestle or food processor and grind to a smooth paste—add a little water if necessary.

Heat a wok over high heat, add the oil, and swirl to coat. Stir in the paste and cook for 1 minute or until fragrant. Add the beans, stir-fry for 2 minutes, then reduce the heat to low. Cover and steam for 2 minutes. Increase the heat to high, add the fish sauce, sugar, and kecap manis, and stir-fry for 1 minute. Toss the noodles through the bean mixture for 1–2 minutes or until heated. Drizzle with the lime juice. Divide among serving bowls. If you wish, serve with lime wedges and garnish with the crisp fried onion flakes and chili slices.

Serves 4

Water spinach in flames

4 cloves garlic, crushed
2 medium fresh green chilies,
  finely sliced
1 tablespoon black bean sauce
2 tablespoons fish sauce
2 teaspoons sugar
2 tablespoons vegetable oil
1 lb. water spinach, cut into
  1¼-in. pieces (see Note)

Place the garlic, chilies, black bean sauce, fish sauce, and sugar in a bowl and mix together well.

Heat a wok over high heat, add the oil, and swirl to coat. Add the spinach and stir-fry for 1 minute or until wilted slightly. Add the sauce and stir-fry for 30 seconds or until the spinach leaves are coated. Serve immediately.

Serves 4

Note: Regular spinach can be used instead of the water spinach.

Lamb with scallions

1¼ lbs. lean lamb fillets, sliced across
the grain into very thin slices
1 tablespoon Chinese rice wine
or dry sherry
¼ cup soy sauce
½ teaspoon white pepper
6 scallions
1½ cups long-grain rice
2 tablespoons vegetable oil
1½ lbs. choy sum, cut into
4-in. pieces
3 cloves garlic, crushed
1 tablespoon Chinese black vinegar
1 teaspoon sesame oil

Put the lamb in a nonmetallic bowl with the rice wine, 1 tablespoon soy sauce, ½ teaspoon salt, and the white pepper, and mix. Cover and chill for 10 minutes. Slice the scallions diagonally into 1½-in. pieces.

Bring a large saucepan of water to a boil. Add the rice and cook for 12 minutes, stirring occasionally. Drain.

Heat a wok over high heat, add ½ tablespoon oil, and swirl to coat. Add the choy sum, and stir-fry. Add 1 clove garlic and 1 tablespoon soy sauce. Cook for 3 minutes or until crisp. Take the wok off the heat, remove the greens, and keep warm.

Wipe out the wok and heat over high heat, then add 1 tablespoon oil to coat. Add the lamb in batches and stir-fry over high heat for 1–2 minutes or until brown. Remove from the wok.

Add more oil to the wok if necessary. Add the scallions and remaining garlic and stir-fry for 1–2 minutes. Combine the vinegar, sesame oil, and the remaining soy sauce. Pour into the wok, stirring for 1 minute. Return the lamb to the wok and stir-fry for another minute or until combined and heated through. Serve immediately with the stir-fried greens and rice.

Serves 4

Eggplant and buckwheat noodle salad

1/4 oz. dried shiitake mushrooms
3/4 lb. buckwheat (soba) noodles
2 teaspoons sesame oil
3 tablespoons tahini
1 tablespoon light soy sauce
1 tablespoon dark soy sauce
1 tablespoon honey
2 tablespoons lemon juice
3 tablespoons peanut oil
2 Japanese eggplants, cut into
  very thin strips
2 carrots, julienned
10 scallions, cut diagonally
6 fresh shiitake mushrooms,
  thinly sliced
1 cup roughly chopped cilantro leaves

Soak the dried shiitake mushrooms in 1/2 cup hot water for 10 minutes. Drain, reserving the liquid. Discard the woody stems and finely slice the caps.

Cook the noodles in a saucepan of boiling water for 5 minutes or until tender. Drain. Rinse under cold water, then toss with 1 teaspoon of the sesame oil.

Combine the tahini, light and dark soy sauces, honey, lemon juice, 2 tablespoons of the reserved mushroom liquid, and the remaining sesame oil in a food processor until smooth.

Heat 2 tablespoons of the peanut oil in a wok over high heat. Add the eggplant and cook, turning often, for 4–5 minutes or until soft and golden. Drain on paper towels.

Heat the remaining oil. Add the carrots, scallions, and fresh and dried mushrooms. Cook, stirring constantly, for 1–2 minutes or until just softened. Remove from the heat and toss with the noodles, eggplant, and dressing. Garnish with the cilantro.

Serves 4–6

Shrimp and rice noodle salad

Dressing
2 tablespoons dark soy sauce
1 tablespoon fish sauce
2 tablespoons lime juice
1 teaspoon grated lime zest
1 teaspoon sugar
1 fresh red chili, seeded and
  finely chopped
2 teaspoons finely chopped
  fresh ginger

5 oz. dried rice vermicelli
1 cup snow peas, trimmed and
  cut in half widthwise
3 tablespoons peanut oil
2/3 cup raw cashews, chopped
24 large shrimp, peeled, deveined,
  and tails intact
1/2 cup fresh mint, chopped
1/2 cup cilantro leaves, chopped

To make the dressing, combine the ingredients in a small bowl.

Soak the noodles in boiling water for 6–7 minutes. Drain and set aside.

Blanch the snow peas in boiling, salted water for 10 seconds. Drain and rinse in cold water.

Heat the oil in a wok and swirl to coat. When hot, add the cashews and stir-fry for 2–3 minutes or until golden. Remove with a slotted spoon and drain on paper towels. Add the shrimp to the wok and cook over high heat, stirring constantly, for 2–3 minutes or until just pink. Transfer to a large bowl, pour on the dressing, and toss. Chill.

Add the noodles, snow peas, mint, cilantro, and cashews, toss well, and serve immediately.

Serves 4

Stir-fried mixed vegetables

2 tablespoons vegetable oil
4 scallions, cut into 1¼-in. pieces
3 cloves garlic, crushed
1 fresh red chili, seeded and sliced
¾ cup button mushrooms, quartered
¼ cup Chinese cabbage,
  roughly chopped
2 tablespoons soy sauce
1 teaspoon fish sauce
1 tablespoon oyster sauce
¼ cup vegetable stock
½ teaspoon grated palm sugar or
  brown sugar
1½ cups snow peas
1¼ cups small cauliflower florets
2½ cups small broccoli florets
fresh cilantro leaves, chopped

Heat a wok until very hot, add the oil, and swirl to coat. Add the scallions, garlic, and chili. Stir-fry for 20 seconds. Add the mushrooms and cabbage and stir-fry for 1 minute.

Stir in the sauces, stock, sugar, snow peas, cauliflower, and broccoli. Cook for 2 minutes or until tender. Garnish with the cilantro leaves.

Serves 6

Lemongrass beef

1 1/2 cups long-grain rice
3 cloves garlic, finely chopped
1 tablespoon grated fresh ginger
4 lemongrass stalks (white part only),
  finely chopped
2 1/2 tablespoons vegetable oil
1 1/4 lbs. lean rump steak, trimmed and
  sliced thinly across the grain
1 tablespoon lime juice
1–2 tablespoons fish sauce
2 tablespoons kecap manis
1 large red onion, cut into
  small wedges
1 2/3 lbs. green beans, sliced
  diagonally into 2-in. pieces

Bring a large saucepan of water to
a boil. Add the rice and cook for
12 minutes, stirring occasionally.
Drain well.

Meanwhile, combine the garlic,
ginger, lemongrass, and 2 teaspoons
of the oil in a nonmetallic bowl.
Add the beef, then marinate for
10 minutes. Combine the lime juice,
fish sauce, and kecap manis.

Heat a wok until very hot, add
1 tablespoon oil, and swirl to coat.
Stir-fry the beef in batches for
2–3 minutes or until browned.
Remove from the wok.

Reheat the wok to very hot, heat the
remaining oil, then add the onion and
stir-fry for 2 minutes. Add the beans
and cook for another 2 minutes, then
return the beef to the wok. Pour in the
fish sauce mixture and cook until
heated through. Serve with the rice.

Serves 4

Caramel pork and squash stir-fry

1¼ cups jasmine rice
1-lb. pork fillet, thinly sliced
2 cloves garlic, crushed
2–3 tablespoons peanut oil
10 oz. butternut squash, cut into
  small chunks
⅓ cup light brown sugar
¼ cup fish sauce
¼ cup rice vinegar
2 tablespoons chopped cilantro
  leaves
2½ lbs. mixed Asian greens
  (bok choy, choy sum, gai larn)

Bring a large saucepan of water to a boil. Add the rice and cook for 12 minutes, stirring occasionally. Drain.

Combine the pork with the garlic and 2 teaspoons of the peanut oil. Season with salt and plenty of pepper.

Heat a wok until very hot, add 1 tablespoon oil, and swirl to coat. When just starting to smoke, stir-fry the pork in two batches for 1 minute per batch or until the meat changes color. Transfer to a plate. Add the remaining oil to the wok and stir-fry the squash for 4 minutes or until tender but not falling apart. Remove and add to the pork.

Combine the sugar, fish sauce, rice vinegar, and ½ cup water in the wok and boil for 10 minutes or until syrupy. Return the pork and squash to the wok and stir for 1 minute or until well coated and heated through. Stir in the cilantro.

Put the mixed Asian greens in a paper-lined bamboo steamer over a wok of simmering water for 3 minutes or until wilted. Serve immediately with the stir-fry and rice.

Serves 4

Tofu, snow pea, and mushroom stir-fry

1 1/4 cups jasmine rice
1/4 cup peanut oil
1 1/4 lbs. firm tofu, drained, cut
  into 3/4-in. cubes
2 teaspoons sambal oelek
  or chili paste
2 cloves garlic, finely chopped
3/4 lb. fresh Asian mushrooms, sliced
  (shiitake, oyster, or black fungus)
3 cups snow peas, trimmed
1/4 cup kecap manis

Bring a large saucepan of water to a boil. Add the rice and cook for 12 minutes, stirring occasionally. Drain well.

Meanwhile, heat a wok until very hot. Add 2 tablespoons of the oil and swirl to coat. Stir-fry the tofu in two batches for 2–3 minutes or until lightly browned, then transfer to a plate.

Add the remaining oil to the wok, add the sambal oelek, garlic, mushrooms, snow peas, and 1 tablespoon water, and stir-fry for 1–2 minutes or until the vegetables are almost cooked but still crunchy.

Return the tofu to the wok, add the kecap manis, and stir-fry for a minute or until heated through and combined. Serve immediately with the rice.

Serves 4

Ginger chicken stir-fry with Hokkien noodles

2½ tablespoons finely shredded
  fresh ginger
¼ cup mirin
2 tablespoons soy sauce
1¼ lbs. chicken tenderloins or
  boneless chicken breasts, cut
  diagonally into thin strips
¾ cup fresh baby corn
¾ lb. choy sum
1⅔ cups fresh oyster mushrooms
1 lb. Hokkien noodles, gently
  separated
2 tablespoons vegetable oil
2 tablespoons oyster sauce

Combine the ginger, mirin, and soy sauce in a nonmetallic bowl. Add the chicken, coat well, then marinate while preparing the vegetables.

Cut the corn in half lengthwise. Trim the ends off the choy sum and cut into 2½-in. pieces. If the mushrooms are very large, cut them in half. Soak the noodles in boiling water in a large heatproof bowl for 5 minutes. Drain and rinse under cold running water.

Heat a wok until very hot, add 1 tablespoon of the oil, and swirl to coat. Remove the chicken from the marinade with a slotted spoon and cook in two batches over very high heat for 2 minutes or until brown and just cooked. Remove from the wok.

Add the remaining oil to the wok and stir-fry the mushrooms and corn for 1–2 minutes or until just softened. Add the remaining marinade, bring to a boil, then add the chicken, choy sum, and noodles. Stir in the oyster sauce and cook, tossing well, for 1–2 minutes or until the choy sum has wilted slightly and the noodles are warmed through.

Serves 4

Shrimp rice noodle rolls

1 tablespoon peanut oil
2 cloves garlic, crushed
2 cups fresh shiitake mushrooms,
thinly sliced
5 scallions, chopped
1/3 cup drained and chopped water
chestnuts
3/4 cup fresh baby corn, roughly
chopped
1 1/4 lbs. medium shrimp, peeled,
deveined, and roughly chopped
1 lb. fresh rice noodle rolls
vegetable oil, for brushing

Sauce
1/4 cup light soy sauce
2 teaspoons sesame oil
1 teaspoon grated fresh ginger
1 teaspoon sugar
2 tablespoons Chinese rice wine

Heat a wok over high heat, add the oil, and swirl to coat. Add the garlic and mushrooms and stir-fry for 1 minute or until soft. Add the scallions, water chestnuts, corn, and shrimp. Cook for 2 minutes or until the corn is just tender and the shrimp begin to turn pink.

Carefully unroll the rice noodle roll and cut it in half. You need two 6 1/2 x 9 1/2-in. rectangles. Place 1/4 cup of the shrimp mixture along one short end of each rectangle, leaving a 1 1/4-in. border. Fold both sides of the noodle roll toward the center, then roll up like a spring roll. Cover with a damp kitchen towel and repeat with the remaining noodle rolls and shrimp mixture.

Line a bamboo steamer with waxed paper, brush with a little oil, then place the rolls in, seam-side down. Place the steamer over a wok filled with simmering water and steam for 4–5 minutes or until the shrimp are cooked through.

Meanwhile, place the soy sauce, sesame oil, ginger, sugar, and rice wine in a small saucepan and stir over medium heat to warm through. Place the rolls on a platter and drizzle with the sauce just before serving.

Serves 4

Udon noodle stir-fry with miso dressing

1 tablespoon white miso
1 tablespoon Japanese soy sauce
2 tablespoons sake
1/2 teaspoon sugar
3/4 lb. fresh udon noodles
1 tablespoon peanut oil
5 scallions, cut into 2-in. pieces
1 red pepper, thinly sliced
1 cup fresh shiitake mushrooms, sliced
1 1/2 cups snow peas, sliced lengthwise into strips

Combine the miso with the soy sauce to form a smooth paste. Add the sake and sugar and mix well.

Cook the udon noodles in a large saucepan of boiling, salted water for 1–2 minutes or until tender and plump. Drain and rinse under cold water.

Heat the oil in a wok over high heat and swirl to coat. Add the scallions and pepper and toss frequently for 1–2 minutes or until softened slightly. Add the mushrooms and snow peas and stir-fry for 2–3 minutes or until tender.

Add the noodles and miso mixture to the wok and toss until well combined. Serve immediately.

Serves 4

Noodle tempura with wasabi dressing

Wasabi dressing
1/2 teaspoon wasabi paste
1 1/2 tablespoons Japanese soy sauce
3 tablespoons mirin

3 oz. dried ramen noodles
1 carrot, grated
2 nori sheets, shredded
2 scallions, finely sliced
1 1/4 cups tempura flour
1 cup ice water
vegetable oil, for deep-frying

Mix the wasabi paste and a little of the soy sauce to make a smooth paste. Add the mirin and remaining soy sauce and stir until there are no lumps.

Cook the noodles in a large saucepan of boiling salted water for 5 minutes or until tender. Drain and rinse under cold water. Cut into 2-in. pieces with scissors. Transfer to a bowl. Mix in the carrot, nori, and scallions. Chill.

Place the tempura flour in a large bowl and make a well in the center. Pour in the ice water and stir gently until the flour and water are just combined (the batter should still be a little lumpy).

Fill a wok one-third full of oil and heat to 350°F or until a cube of bread dropped into the oil browns in 15 seconds. Combine the noodle mixture and tempura batter, tossing lightly. Spoon 1/4 cup of the mixture into the oil, and using a fork or chopsticks, quickly and carefully spread the mixture out a little. Cook for 2–3 minutes, turning occasionally, or until golden and cooked through. Remove and drain. Keep warm in the oven while you repeat with the remaining mixture. Serve immediately with the wasabi dressing.

Serves 4

Chinese omelettes with mushroom sauce

6 whole dried shiitake mushrooms
6 eggs, lightly beaten
4 scallions, thinly sliced
1 small red pepper, thinly sliced
1 cup bean sprouts
2 teaspoons sesame oil
1 teaspoon soy sauce
1 tablespoon vegetable oil
1½ tablespoons vegetable oil, extra
2 cloves garlic, crushed
1 cup chicken stock
1 tablespoon oyster sauce
2 teaspoons soy sauce
1 teaspoon sugar
2 scallions, sliced diagonally, extra
2 teaspoons cornstarch

Place the mushrooms in a heatproof bowl, cover with boiling water, and soak for 15 minutes. Drain, discard the stems, and thinly slice the caps.

Meanwhile, mix the egg, scallions, pepper, bean sprouts, sesame oil, and soy sauce in a bowl. Season.

Heat a wok over high heat, add 2 teaspoons oil, and swirl to coat. Add a quarter of the egg mixture to the wok, swirl to coat evenly, and cook for 1–2 minutes or until almost set. Turn over and cook for 1 minute or until brown. Remove and keep warm. Repeat with the remaining mixture, adding more oil if necessary.

Reheat the wok over high heat, add the extra oil, and swirl. Add the garlic and mushrooms and cook for 1 minute. Add the stock, oyster sauce, soy sauce, sugar, and extra scallions. Bring to a boil, then reduce the heat and simmer for 1 minute. Combine the cornstarch with 1 tablespoon water, add to the wok, and simmer for 2 minutes or until thickened slightly. Serve the omelettes topped with the sauce.

Serves 2–4

Stir-fried lamb with mint, chilies, and Shanghai noodles

3/4 lb. Shanghai noodles
1 teaspoon sesame oil
2 tablespoons peanut oil
7 oz. boneless lamb steak, cut into
  thin strips
2 cloves garlic, crushed
2 fresh red chilies, seeded and
  finely sliced
1 tablespoon oyster sauce
2 teaspoons palm sugar or
  brown sugar
2 tablespoons fish sauce
2 tablespoons lime juice
1/2 cup fresh mint, chopped
lime wedges, to garnish

Cook the noodles in a large saucepan of boiling water for 4–5 minutes. Drain, then rinse in cold water. Add the sesame oil and toss through.

Heat the peanut oil in a wok over high heat. Add the lamb and cook in batches for 1–2 minutes or until just browned. Return all the meat to the wok and add the garlic and chilies. Cook for 30 seconds, then add the oyster sauce, sugar, fish sauce, lime juice, and noodles. Cook for another 2–3 minutes or until the noodles are warm. Stir in the mint and serve immediately with the lime wedges.

Serves 4–6

Chinese beef and asparagus with oyster sauce

1 lb. 2 oz. lean beef fillet, thinly sliced
  across the grain
1 tablespoon light soy sauce
1/2 teaspoon sesame oil
1 tablespoon Chinese rice wine
2 1/2 tablespoons vegetable oil
3 1/2 oz. fresh, thin asparagus, cut into
  thirds diagonally
3 cloves garlic, crushed
2 teaspoons julienned fresh ginger
1/4 cup chicken stock
2–3 tablespoons oyster sauce

Place the beef slices in a nonmetallic bowl with the soy sauce, sesame oil, and 2 teaspoons of the rice wine. Cover and marinate for 15 minutes.

Heat a wok over high heat, add 1 tablespoon of the vegetable oil, and swirl to coat the side of the wok. When the oil is hot but not smoking, add the asparagus and stir-fry for 1–2 minutes. Remove from the wok.

Add another tablespoon of oil to the wok, and when hot, add the beef in two batches, stir-frying each batch for 1–2 minutes or until cooked. Remove the meat from the wok.

Add the remaining oil to the wok, and when hot, add the garlic and ginger and stir-fry for 1 minute or until fragrant. Pour the stock, oyster sauce, and remaining rice wine into the wok, bring to a boil, and boil rapidly for 1–2 minutes or until the sauce is slightly reduced. Return the beef and asparagus to the wok and stir-fry for an additional minute or until heated through and coated in the sauce. Serve immediately with steamed rice.

Serves 4

Satay chicken stir-fry

1 1/2 cups jasmine rice
1 1/2 tablespoons peanut oil
6 scallions, cut into 1 1/4-in. pieces
1 lb. 10 oz. chicken breasts, thinly
    sliced diagonally
1–1 1/2 tablespoons Thai red
    curry paste
1/3 cup crunchy peanut butter
1 cup coconut milk
2 teaspoons light brown sugar
1 1/2 tablespoons lime juice

Bring a large saucepan of water to a boil. Add the rice and cook for 12 minutes, stirring occasionally. Drain well.

Meanwhile, heat a wok until very hot, add 1 teaspoon of the peanut oil, and swirl to coat. When hot, add the scallions and stir-fry for 30 seconds or until softened slightly. Remove from the wok. Add a little extra peanut oil to the wok as needed and stir-fry the chicken in three batches for 1 minute per batch or until the meat just changes color. Remove from the wok.

Add a little more oil to the wok, add the curry paste, and stir-fry for 1 minute or until fragrant. Add the peanut butter, coconut milk, sugar, and 1 cup water and stir well. Bring to a boil and boil for 3–4 minutes or until thickened and the oil starts to separate—reduce the heat slightly if the sauce spits. Return the chicken and the scallions to the wok, stir well, and cook for 2 minutes or until heated through. Stir in the lime juice and season. Serve at once with the rice and a crisp green salad.

Serves 4

Calamari with green peppercorns

1 1/4 lbs. squid bodies
2 teaspoons chopped cilantro root
3 cloves garlic, crushed
4 tablespoons vegetable oil
3/4 oz. Thai green peppercorns on
  the stem, in brine, or lightly
  crushed fresh peppercorns
2 tablespoons Thai mushroom
  soy sauce
1/2 teaspoon grated palm sugar or
  brown sugar
2/3 cup fresh Thai basil
green peppercorns, extra,
  to garnish

Cut the squid bodies in half lengthwise. Cut a crisscross pattern on the inside of the squid. Cut into 1 1/2-in. squares.

Place the cilantro root, 1 clove garlic, and 1 tablespoon oil in a food processor and process to form a smooth paste. Mix together the paste and squid pieces, cover, and allow to marinate for 30 minutes.

Heat a wok over high heat, add the remaining oil, and swirl to coat the side. Add the squid pieces and the remaining garlic and stir-fry for 1 minute. Add the peppercorns and stir-fry for another 2 minutes or until the squid is just cooked—it will toughen if overcooked. Add the soy sauce and sugar and stir until the sugar has dissolved. Serve immediately, garnished with Thai basil and extra green peppercorns.

Serves 4

Note: Although the squid takes a while to marinate, the actual cooking time is not long.

Grill

Tuna steaks on cilantro noodles

¼ cup lime juice
2 tablespoons fish sauce
2 tablespoons sweet chili sauce
2 teaspoons grated palm sugar or
  brown sugar
1 teaspoon sesame oil
1 clove garlic, finely chopped
1 tablespoon extra-virgin olive oil
4 5-oz. tuna steaks, at room
  temperature
6 oz. thin, dried wheat noodles
6 scallions, thinly sliced
¾ cup chopped cilantro leaves
lime wedges, to garnish

To make the dressing, place the lime juice, fish sauce, chili sauce, sugar, sesame oil, and garlic in a small bowl and mix together.

Heat the olive oil in a ridged cast-iron grill pan. Add the tuna steaks and cook over high heat for 2 minutes each side or until cooked to your liking. Transfer the steaks to a warm plate, cover, and keep warm.

Place the noodles in a large saucepan of lightly salted, rapidly boiling water and return to a boil. Cook for 4 minutes or until the noodles are tender. Drain well. Add half each of the dressing, scallions, and cilantro to the noodles and gently toss together.

Either cut the tuna into even-size cubes or slice it.

Place the noodles on serving plates and top with the tuna. Mix the remaining dressing with the scallions and cilantro and drizzle over the tuna. Garnish with lime wedges.

Serves 4

Note: If you prefer, you can serve the tuna steaks whole rather than cutting them into cubes. If serving whole, they look better served with the noodles on the side.

Barbecued chermoula shrimp

2 lbs. medium shrimp
3 teaspoons hot paprika
2 teaspoons ground cumin
1 cup firmly packed fresh
  Italian parsley
½ cup firmly packed fresh cilantro
  leaves
½ cup lemon juice
⅔ cup extra-virgin olive oil
1½ cups couscous
1 tablespoon grated lemon zest
lemon wedges, to serve

Peel the shrimp, leaving the tails intact. Gently pull out the dark vein from the backs, starting at the head end. Place the shrimp in a large bowl. Dry-fry the paprika and cumin in a frying pan for 1 minute or until fragrant. Remove from the heat.

Blend or process the spices, parsley, cilantro, lemon juice, and ½ cup of the oil until finely chopped. Add a little salt and pepper. Pour over the shrimp and mix well, then cover with plastic wrap and refrigerate for 10 minutes. Heat a ridged cast-iron grill pan until hot.

Meanwhile, to cook the couscous, bring 1 cup water to a boil in a saucepan, then stir in the couscous, lemon zest, the remaining oil, and ¼ teaspoon salt. Remove from the heat, cover, and leave for 5 minutes. Fluff the couscous with a fork, adding a little extra olive oil if needed.

Cook the shrimp on the grill pan for about 3–4 minutes or until cooked through, turning and brushing with extra marinade while cooking (be careful not to overcook). Serve the shrimp on a bed of couscous, with a lemon wedge.

Serves 4

Paprika lamb kabobs with skordalia

2 lbs. lamb fillets, cut into
  3/4-inch cubes
1 tablespoon sweet paprika
1 tablespoon hot paprika
1/2 cup lemon juice
1/2 cup olive oil
3 large russet potatoes, cut into large
  cubes
3–4 cloves garlic, crushed, with
  a pinch of salt
10 handfuls spinach leaves
lemon wedges, to serve

Soak twelve wooden skewers in water for 30 minutes. Thread six lamb cubes onto each, then place in a nonmetallic, rectangular dish large enough to hold all the skewers in one layer.

Combine the sweet and hot paprika, 1/3 cup lemon juice, and 1/4 cup oil in a small, nonmetallic pitcher. Pour over the skewers. Season. Cover and chill.

For the skordalia, boil the potatoes for 20 minutes or until tender. Drain. Put in a food processor with the garlic and 1 tablespoon of the lemon juice. With the motor running, slowly add the remaining oil in a thin stream and continue blending for 30–60 seconds or until all the oil is incorporated— avoid overprocessing, as the mixture will become gluey. Season. Set aside.

Heat a ridged cast-iron grill pan and brush with oil. Cook the skewers for 3–4 minutes each side for medium-rare or 5–6 minutes for well done.

Wash the spinach and put in a pan with just the water clinging to the leaves. Cook, covered, over medium heat for 1–2 minutes or until wilted. Remove and stir in the remaining lemon juice. Serve the kabobs with skordalia, spinach, and lemon wedges.

Serves 4

Grilled haloumi and roast vegetable salad

4 slender eggplants, cut in half, then
  halved lengthwise
1 red pepper, halved, thickly sliced
4 small zucchini, cut in half, then
  halved lengthwise
1/3 cup olive oil
2 cloves garlic, crushed
6 oz. haloumi cheese, cut into
  1/4-inch-thick slices
3 cups baby spinach leaves, trimmed
1 tablespoon balsamic vinegar

Preheat the oven to 425°F. Place the vegetables in a large bowl, add 1/4 cup olive oil and the garlic, season, and toss well to combine. Place the vegetables in a flameproof dish in a single layer. Roast for 20–30 minutes or until tender and browned around the edges.

Meanwhile, lightly brush a ridged cast-iron grill pan or heavy-bottomed frying pan with oil and cook the haloumi slices for 1–2 minutes on each side.

Place the spinach leaves on four serving plates. Top with the roast vegetables and haloumi. Place the remaining oil in a small pitcher, add the vinegar, and whisk to combine, then pour over the vegetables and haloumi. Serve immediately, warm or at room temperature, with lots of crusty bread.

Serves 4

Note: You can use any roasted vegetable, such as orange sweet potatoes, leeks, or Roma tomatoes.

Linguine with basil and lemon seafood

16 medium shrimp, peeled and
  deveined, with tails intact
3/4 lb. squid rings
1/2 cup extra-virgin olive oil
1/3 cup lemon juice
3 cloves garlic, crushed
1/2 teaspoon chili flakes
3 tablespoons chopped fresh basil
13 oz. linguine
1 teaspoon grated lemon zest

Place the shrimp and squid in a nonmetallic dish. To make the dressing, combine the olive oil and lemon juice in a small pitcher, then pour 1/4 cup into a small bowl, reserving the rest. Stir the garlic, chili flakes, and 2 tablespoons of the basil into the bowl, pour over the seafood, and mix to coat well. Cover with plastic wrap and marinate in the refrigerator for 5–10 minutes.

Cook the pasta in a large saucepan of rapidly boiling salted water according to the packet instructions until al dente. Drain. Return to the saucepan.

Meanwhile, preheat a ridged cast-iron grill pan to high and brush with oil. Remove the shrimp from the marinade with tongs and cook for 2–3 minutes on each side or until pink and cooked through. Remove. Add the squid in batches and cook, turning once, for 1–3 minutes, or until opaque and cooked through—be careful not to overcrowd the ridged pan.

Transfer the pasta to a large serving bowl, then add the seafood, lemon zest, and reserved dressing, and gently toss together until the linguine is well coated. Garnish with the remaining basil and season to taste. Serve with an arugula salad.

Serves 4

White bean salad with tuna

1 cup dried cannellini beans
  or 1 14-oz. can cannellini beans,
  rinsed and drained well
2 fresh bay leaves
1 large clove garlic, smashed
3/4 lb. green beans, trimmed
2 small baby fennel, thinly sliced
1/2 small red onion, very thinly sliced
1 cup fresh Italian parsley,
  roughly chopped
1 tablespoon olive oil
2 fresh tuna steaks (6 oz. each)
1/3 cup lemon juice
1 clove garlic, extra, finely chopped
1 small, fresh red chili, seeds
  removed, finely chopped
1 teaspoon sugar
1 tablespoon lemon zest
1/2 cup extra-virgin olive oil

If using dried beans, put them in a bowl, cover with cold water, allowing room for the beans to expand, and leave for at least 8 hours.

Rinse the beans well and transfer them to a saucepan. Cover with cold water, add the torn bay leaves and smashed garlic, and simmer for 20–25 minutes or until tender. Drain.

Cook the green beans in boiling water for 1–2 minutes or until tender, then rinse under cold water. Mix with the fennel, onion, and parsley in a bowl.

Brush the oil over the tuna fillets and broil under high heat for 2 minutes on each side or until still pink in the center. Remove, rest for 2–3 minutes, then cut into 1 1/4-inch chunks. Add to the green bean mixture and toss.

Mix the lemon juice, garlic, chili, sugar, and lemon zest together. Whisk in the extra-virgin olive oil and season with salt and pepper. Toss gently through the salad.

Serves 4–6

Vegetable salad with balsamic dressing

4 baby eggplants
5 Roma tomatoes
2 red peppers
1 green pepper
2 zucchini
1/2 cup olive oil
12 baby bocconcini
1/4 cup green olives
1 clove garlic, finely chopped
3 teaspoons baby capers
1/2 teaspoon sugar
2 tablespoons balsamic vinegar

Cut the eggplants and tomatoes in half lengthwise. Cut the red and green peppers in half lengthwise, remove the seeds and membrane, then cut each half into three pieces. Thinly slice the zucchini diagonally.

Preheat a ridged cast-iron grill pan. Add 1 tablespoon of oil and cook a quarter of the vegetables (cook the tomatoes cut-side down first) for about 2–3 minutes or until marked and golden. Place in a bowl.

Cook the remaining vegetables in batches until tender, adding more oil as needed. Transfer to the bowl and add the baby bocconcini. Mix the olives, garlic, capers, sugar, vinegar, and remaining oil (about 2 tablespoons). Pour over the salad and toss. Season with pepper.

Serves 4–6

Lamb chops with mint gremolata

4 tablespoons fresh mint leaves
1 tablespoon fresh Italian parsley
2 cloves garlic
1½ tablespoons lemon zest (white pith removed), cut into thin strips
2 tablespoons extra-virgin olive oil
8 French-trimmed lamb chops
2 carrots
2 zucchini
1 tablespoon lemon juice

To make the gremolata, finely chop the mint, parsley, garlic and lemon strips, then combine well.

Heat a ridged cast-iron grill pan until very hot. Lightly brush with 1 tablespoon of the oil. Cook the chops over medium heat for 2 minutes on each side or until cooked to your liking. Remove the chops and cover to keep warm.

Trim the ends from the carrots and zucchini and, using a sharp vegetable peeler, peel the vegetables lengthwise into ribbons. Heat the remaining oil in a large saucepan, add the vegetables, and toss over medium heat for 3–5 minutes or until sautéed but tender.

Divide the chops among the serving plates, sprinkle the chops with the gremolata, and drizzle with the lemon juice. Serve with the vegetable ribbons.

Serves 4

Vegetable skewers with basil couscous

5 thin zucchini, cut into ¾-inch cubes
5 slender eggplants, cut into
  ¾-inch cubes
12 button mushrooms, halved
2 red peppers, cut into ½-inch cubes
8 oz. kefalotyri cheese, cut into
  ¾-inch-thick pieces
⅓ cup lemon juice
2 garlic cloves, finely chopped
5 tablespoons finely chopped
  fresh basil
½ cup extra-virgin olive oil
1 cup couscous
1 teaspoon grated lemon zest

Soak twelve wooden skewers in water for 30 minutes. Thread alternate pieces of vegetables and kefalotyri, starting and finishing with a piece of pepper and using two pieces of kefalotyri per skewer. Place in a nonmetallic dish that will hold them in one layer.

Combine the lemon juice, garlic, 4 tablespoons basil, and ½ cup oil in a nonmetallic bowl. Season. Pour two thirds of the marinade over the skewers, reserving the remainder. Turn to coat, cover with plastic wrap and marinate for at least 5 minutes.

Place the couscous, lemon zest, and 1½ cups boiling water in a large heatproof bowl. Let stand for 5 minutes or until all the water has been absorbed. Add the remaining oil and basil, then fluff gently with a fork to separate the grains. Cover.

Heat a ridged cast-iron grill pan to medium-high. Cook the skewers, brushing often with the leftover marinade, for 4–5 minutes on each side or until the vegetables are cooked and the cheese browns.

Divide the couscous and skewers among serving plates. Season, then drizzle with the reserved marinade.

Serves 4

Barbecued Asian spareribs with scallion rice

2 lbs. pork spareribs, cut into
  sections of 4–5 ribs
¼ cup hoisin sauce
1 tablespoon Chinese rice wine
  or dry sherry
¼ cup soy sauce
2 cloves garlic, chopped
2 tablespoons vegetable oil
3 spring onions, finely chopped
1 tablespoon grated fresh ginger
1¼ cups jasmine rice
1¼ lb. baby bok choy, leaves
  separated

Place the ribs in a nonmetallic bowl. Combine the hoisin sauce, rice wine, soy sauce, garlic, 1 tablespoon oil, 2 tablespoons scallions, and half the ginger. Pour over the ribs and marinate for at least 10 minutes or overnight in the refrigerator.

Bring a large saucepan of water to a boil. Add the rice and cook for 12 minutes, stirring occasionally. Drain.

Heat the remaining oil in a small pan over medium-low heat. When the oil is warm but not smoking, remove the saucepan from the heat and add the rest of the scallions and ginger. Stir in ¼ teaspoon salt. Stir through the rice.

Heat a ridged cast-iron grill pan and brush with oil. Remove the ribs from the marinade, reserving the marinade. Cook the ribs in batches for 8–10 minutes on each side or until cooked through, basting with the marinade during cooking.

Before the ribs are cooked, bring the reserved marinade to a boil in a saucepan (add ⅓ cup water if needed). Boil for 2 minutes, then add the bok choy. Cover and cook for 1–2 minutes or until just wilted. Serve the ribs with the rice and bok choy and drizzle with the marinade.

Serves 4

Angel-hair pasta with scallops and arugula

3/4 lb. angel-hair pasta
1/3 cup butter
3 cloves garlic, crushed
24 scallops, without roe
5 handfuls baby arugula leaves
2 teaspoons finely grated lemon zest
1/4 cup lemon juice
3/4 cup sun-dried tomatoes,
  thinly sliced
1/3 cup shaved Parmesan

Cook the pasta in a large saucepan of boiling water until al dente. Meanwhile, melt the butter in a small saucepan, add the garlic, and cook over low heat, stirring, for 1 minute. Remove from the heat.

Heat a lightly greased, ridged cast-iron grill pan over high heat and cook the scallops, brushing occasionally with some of the garlic butter, for 1–2 minutes on each side or until cooked. Set aside and keep warm.

Drain the pasta and return to the saucepan with the remaining garlic butter, the arugula, lemon zest, lemon juice, and tomatoes and toss until combined. Divide among four serving plates and top with the scallops. Season to taste and sprinkle with Parmesan.

Serves 4

Rosemary and red wine steaks with barbecued vegetables

12 small new potatoes
1/4 cup extra-virgin olive oil
1 tablespoon finely chopped
  fresh rosemary
6 cloves garlic, sliced
sea salt, to season
4 large portobello mushrooms
12 asparagus spears
1 cup red wine
4 1/2-lb. beef rib-eye steaks

Heat a ridged cast-iron grill pan until hot. Toss the potatoes with 1 tablespoon of the oil, half the rosemary, and half the garlic, and season with the sea salt. Divide the potatoes among four large sheets of aluminum foil and wrap into neat packages, sealing firmly around the edges. Cook on the grill, turning frequently for 30–40 minutes or until tender.

Meanwhile, brush the mushrooms and asparagus with a little of the remaining oil and set aside.

Combine the red wine with the remaining oil, rosemary, and garlic in a nonmetallic dish. Season with lots of freshly ground black pepper. Add the steaks and coat in the marinade. Allow to marinate for 25 minutes, then drain.

Cook the steaks and mushrooms on the grill until cooked to your liking (this will depend on the thickness of the steak). Transfer the steaks and mushrooms to a plate, cover lightly, and allow to rest. Add the asparagus to the grill, turning regularly for about 2 minutes or until tender. Pierce the potatoes with a skewer to check for doneness. Season. Serve the steaks with the vegetables.

Serves 4

Cajun chicken with fresh tomatoes and corn salsa

2 ears of corn
2 vine-ripened tomatoes, diced
1 cucumber, diced
2 tablespoons roughly chopped
  cilantro leaves
4 6-oz. boneless chicken breasts
¼ cup Cajun seasoning
2 tablespoons lime juice
lime wedges, to serve

Cook the corn in a saucepan of boiling water for 5 minutes or until tender. Remove the kernels with a sharp knife and place in a bowl with the tomatoes, cucumber, and cilantro. Season and mix well.

Heat a ridged cast-iron grill pan to medium heat and brush lightly with oil. Pound each chicken breast between two sheets of plastic wrap with a mallet or rolling pin until ¾ in. thick. Lightly coat the chicken with the Cajun seasoning and shake off any excess. Cook for 5 minutes on each side or until just cooked through.

Just before serving, stir the lime juice into the salsa. Place a chicken breast on each plate and spoon the salsa on the side. Serve with the lime wedges, a green salad, and crusty bread.

Serves 4

Sumac-crusted lamb steaks with baba ghanouj

2 tablespoons extra-virgin olive oil
1½ lbs. small new potatoes
2–3 cloves garlic, crushed
¼ cup lemon juice
1 red pepper, seeded and quartered
   lengthwise
4 6-oz. lamb fillets
1 tablespoon sumac (see Note)
3 tablespoons finely chopped
   fresh Italian parsley
1 cup good-quality baba ghanouj
   (eggplant dip)

Heat the oil in a saucepan big enough to hold the potatoes in one layer. Cook the potatoes and garlic, turning frequently, for 3–5 minutes or until golden. Add the lemon juice and reduce the heat to medium-low. Simmer, covered, for 15–20 minutes or until tender, stirring occasionally. Season well.

Meanwhile, lightly oil a ridged cast-iron grill pan and heat to very hot. Cook the pepper skin-side down for 1–2 minutes or until the skin starts to blister and turn black. Cook the other side for 1–2 minutes. Place the pepper in a plastic bag.

Coat the lamb with sumac. Cook on the ridged pan for 4–5 minutes each side or until cooked to your liking. Remove and cover with foil. Peel the pepper and cut into thin strips.

Stir the parsley through the potatoes. Divide the baba ghanouj among four plates. Cut the lamb diagonally into ½-in. slices and arrange on the baba ghanouj with the pepper. Serve with the potatoes and a salad.

Serves 4

Note: Sumac is available from Middle Eastern markets. If unavailable, use the same amount of ground cumin.

Gnocchi with creamy Gorgonzola and sage sauce

2 1-lb. packages potato gnocchi
¼ cup butter
2 cloves garlic, crushed
½ cup fresh small sage leaves
3½ oz. Gorgonzola cheese
½ cup whipping cream
1 cup grated Parmesan

Preheat the broiler to high. Lightly grease four 1-cup, flameproof, gratin dishes. Cook the gnocchi in a large saucepan of rapidly boiling, salted water according to the package instructions until al dente. Lift the gnocchi out with a slotted spoon, leave to drain, then divide among the prepared dishes.

Melt the butter in a small saucepan over medium heat, add the garlic and sage leaves, and cook for a few minutes or until the leaves start to crispen and the garlic browns a little. Pour the sage butter evenly over the gnocchi in the gratin dishes.

Dot small pats of the Gorgonzola evenly among the gnocchi. Pour the cream over the top of each dish and sprinkle with the Parmesan. Place the dishes under the broiler and cook until the top starts to brown and the gnocchi are heated through. Serve with a fresh green salad.

Serves 4

Note: This can also be cooked in a 4-cup rectangular, flameproof, ceramic dish or round pie dish.

Thai beef skewers with peanut sauce

1 onion, chopped
2 cloves garlic, crushed
2 teaspoons sambal oelek
1 lemongrass stalk, white part only, chopped
2 teaspoons chopped fresh ginger
1 1/2 tablespoons vegetable oil
1 cup coconut cream
1/2 cup crunchy peanut butter
1 1/2 tablespoons fish sauce
2 teaspoons soy sauce
1 tablespoon grated palm sugar or brown sugar
2 tablespoons lime juice
2 tablespoons chopped cilantro leaves
1 1/2-lb. beef round or rump steak, cut into 3/4 x 4-in. pieces
2 teaspoons oil, extra
fresh red chili, chopped, to garnish (optional)
chopped roasted peanuts, to garnish (optional)

Put the onion, garlic, sambal oelek, lemongrass, and ginger in a food processor and process to a smooth paste.

Heat the oil in a saucepan over medium heat, add the paste, and cook, stirring, for 2–3 minutes or until fragrant. Add the coconut cream, peanut butter, fish sauce, soy sauce, sugar, and lime juice and bring to a boil. Reduce the heat and simmer for 5 minutes, then stir in the cilantro.

Meanwhile, thread the meat onto twelve metal skewers and cook in a nonstick frying pan with the extra oil for 2 minutes each side or until cooked to your liking. Serve the skewers on a bed of rice with the sauce and a salad on the side. Garnish with the chopped chili and peanuts, if desired.

Serves 4

Note: If using wooden skewers, soak them for 30 minutes before broiling to keep them from burning.

Lime and cilantro chicken

3 teaspoons finely grated fresh ginger
1/2 cup chopped cilantro leaves
1 1/2 teaspoons grated lime zest
1/3 cup lime juice
4 chicken breasts (1 1/2 lbs. total),
   trimmed
1 1/4 cups jasmine rice
2 tablespoons vegetable oil
3 zucchini, cut into wedges
4 large, flat mushrooms,
   stems trimmed

Combine the ginger, cilantro, lime zest, and 2 tablespoons of the lime juice. Spread 2 teaspoons of the herb mixture over each chicken breast and season well. Marinate for 1 hour. Combine the remaining herb mixture with the remaining lime juice in a screw-top jar. Set aside until needed.

Bring a large saucepan of water to a boil. Add the rice and cook for 12 minutes, stirring occasionally. Drain well.

Meanwhile, heat a ridged cast-iron grill pan to medium and lightly brush with oil. Brush the zucchini and mushrooms with the remaining oil. Place the chicken on the ridged pan and cook on each side for 4–5 minutes or until cooked through. Add the vegetables during the last 5 minutes of cooking, and turn frequently until browned on the outside and just softened. Cover with aluminum foil until ready to serve.

Divide the rice among four serving bowls. Cut the chicken breasts into long, thick strips, then arrange on top of the rice. Shake the dressing well and drizzle over the chicken and serve with the vegetables.

Serves 4

Grilled jumbo shrimp

8 large shrimp (1 1/2 lbs.)
1/3 cup extra-virgin olive oil
3 cloves garlic, crushed
1 tablespoon sweet chili sauce
2 tablespoons lime juice
1/4 cup extra-virgin olive oil, extra
2 tablespoons lime juice, extra
mixed lettuce leaves, to serve

Remove the heads from the shrimp and, using a sharp knife, cut through the center of the shrimp lengthwise to form two halves, leaving the tails and shells intact.

Place the olive oil, 2 crushed garlic cloves, sweet chili sauce, and lime juice in a large bowl and mix together well. Add the shrimp, toss to coat, and marinate for 30 minutes.

Meanwhile, combine the extra oil and lime juice and remaining garlic in a bowl. Heat a ridged cast-iron grill pan until hot. Drain the shrimp and cook cut-side down first, brushing with the marinade, for 1–2 minutes each side or until cooked. Divide the lettuce among four serving plates, place the shrimp on top, and spoon over the dressing. Season and serve.

Serves 4

Barbecued steak with caramelized balsamic onions and mustard crème fraîche

1½ tablespoons whole-grain mustard
1 cup crème fraîche
2 peppers (1 red and 1 yellow),
 seeded and quartered
2 zucchini, trimmed and sliced
 lengthwise into strips
2 tablespoons vegetable oil
2 large red onions, thinly sliced
4 6-oz. rump steaks
2 tablespoons light brown sugar
¼ cup balsamic vinegar

Heat a large, ridged cast-iron grill pan until hot. Combine the mustard and crème fraîche in a bowl. Season, then cover and set aside.

Brush the peppers and zucchini with 1 tablespoon oil. Cook the peppers, turning regularly, for 5 minutes or until tender and slightly charred. Remove and cover with aluminum foil. Repeat with the zucchini.

Heat the remaining oil in the pan, then cook the onion, turning occasionally, for 5–10 minutes or until softened. When nearly soft, push to the side of the pan, then add the steaks and cook on each side for 3–4 minutes (medium-rare) or until cooked to your liking. Remove the steaks, cover with aluminum foil, and allow to rest. Spread the onion over the pan once again, reduce the heat, sprinkle with sugar, and cook for 1–2 minutes or until the sugar has dissolved and the onion appears glossy. Add the vinegar, stirring continuously for 1–2 minutes or until it is absorbed. Remove at once.

Peel the peppers, then divide among serving plates with the zucchini. Place the steaks on top, season, and top with the balsamic onions. Serve with the mustard crème fraîche.

Serves 4

Stuffed mushrooms with spiced couscous

8 portobello mushrooms
1/2 cup instant couscous
1 tablespoon extra-virgin olive oil
1 teaspoon ground cumin
1/4 teaspoon cayenne pepper
2 teaspoons finely grated lemon zest
1/2 cup chicken stock
1 tomato, finely chopped
1 tablespoon lemon juice
2 tablespoons chopped fresh
  Italian parsley
2 tablespoons chopped fresh mint

Peel the mushrooms and remove the stems, then broil them top-side up.

Place the couscous, olive oil, cumin, cayenne pepper, and lemon zest in a bowl. Season, then stir the flavorings through the couscous.

Bring the chicken stock to a boil and stir it into the couscous. Cover and leave for 5 minutes, then fluff the grains with a fork. Stir in the tomato, lemon juice, parsley, and mint. Fill each mushroom with some of the couscous mixture and pack down firmly. Broil until the couscous is golden. Serve hot or cold.

Makes 8

Tandoori chicken with cardamom rice

3/4 cup plain yogurt, plus extra
   for serving
1/4 cup tandoori paste
2 tablespoons lemon juice
2 lbs. boneless chicken breasts, cut
   into 1 1/4-in. cubes
1 tablespoon vegetable oil
1 onion, finely diced
1 1/2 cups long-grain rice
2 cardamom pods, bruised
3 cups hot chicken stock
3/4 lb. spinach leaves

Soak eight wooden skewers in water for 30 minutes to keep them from burning during cooking. Combine the yogurt, tandoori paste, and lemon juice in a nonmetallic dish. Add the chicken and coat well, then cover and marinate for at least 10 minutes.

Meanwhile, heat the oil in a saucepan. Add the onion and cook for 3 minutes, then add the rice and cardamom pods. Cook, stirring often, for 3–5 minutes or until the rice is slightly opaque. Add the stock and bring to a boil. Reduce the heat to low, cover, and cook, without removing the lid, for 15 minutes.

Heat a grill or broiler until very hot. Thread the chicken cubes onto the skewers, leaving the bottom quarter of the skewers empty. Cook on each side for 4–5 minutes or until cooked through.

Wash the spinach and place in a large saucepan with just the water clinging to the leaves. Cook, covered, over medium heat for 1–2 minutes or until the spinach has wilted. Uncover the rice, fluff with a fork, and serve with the spinach, chicken, and extra yogurt.

Serves 4

Lamb pide with garlic and chickpea purée

1 tablespoon lemon juice
1 teaspoon ground cumin
1 tablespoon extra-virgin olive oil
4 trimmed lamb fillets
1 head of garlic
½ cup canned chickpeas, drained
2 teaspoons lemon juice, extra
1 tablespoon low-fat plain yogurt
4 3-oz. pieces Turkish bread or
  focaccia

Mix the lemon juice, cumin, olive oil, and some salt and pepper. Add the lamb fillets and allow to marinate for at least 1 hour.

Preheat the oven to 415°F. Wrap the head of garlic in foil, then roast for 20 minutes or until soft. Cool, then squeeze out the pulp from each clove. Purée the pulp with the chickpeas, extra lemon juice, and low-fat yogurt in a food processor—add a little water to achieve a spreading consistency, if needed. Season.

Broil or barbecue the lamb for 3 minutes on each side or until done to your liking. Broil or toast the bread, then slice through the middle and spread with the chickpea spread. Top with thin slices of the lamb, tomato slices, and arugula leaves.

Serves 4

Grilled baby octopus

3 lbs. baby octopus
1 cup sweet chili sauce
1/3 cup lime juice
1/3 cup fish sauce
1/3 cup light brown sugar
vegetable oil, for grilling
mixed lettuce leaves, to serve
lime wedges, to serve

Cut the head from the octopus and discard. With your fingers, push the hard beak up and out of the body. Rinse, drain, and pat dry.

Place the sweet chili sauce, lime juice, fish sauce, and sugar in a small bowl and mix together well.

Brush a ridged cast-iron grill pan with oil and heat until very hot. Cook the octopus, turning, for 3–4 minutes or until they change color. Brush with a quarter of the sauce during cooking. Do not overcook. Serve immediately on a bed of salad greens with the remaining sauce and the lime wedges.

Serves 4

Oven

Polenta with mushrooms, spinach, and tomatoes

4 Roma tomatoes, halved lengthwise
4 large portobello mushrooms
1/3 cup garlic-flavored oil (see Note)
3 1/2 cups vegetable stock
1 1/4 cups instant polenta
5 oz. goat cheese, chopped
1/2 cup grated Parmesan
10-oz. bag baby spinach leaves

Place the tomatoes and mushrooms in a nonmetallic dish, brush with half the garlic oil, and allow to marinate for 30 minutes. Preheat the oven to 400°F.

Place the tomatoes in a baking dish and bake for 20 minutes. Meanwhile, place the stock in a large saucepan and bring to a boil, add the polenta in a slow steady stream, and cook, stirring, for 10 minutes or until creamy. Stir in the goat cheese and half the Parmesan. Remove from the heat and keep warm.

Heat 1 tablespoon garlic oil in a frying pan, add the mushrooms, and cook, turning once, for 3–4 minutes or until cooked, but not starting to release too much juice. Remove from the pan. Add the remaining oil to the pan, add the spinach, and cook for 3–4 minutes or until just wilted. Spoon the polenta onto four warm serving plates, arrange the spinach on top, then a mushroom, and top with two tomato halves. Sprinkle with the remaining Parmesan and serve.

Serves 4

Note: Instead of buying garlic-flavored oil, you can marinate a crushed garlic clove in 1/3 cup extra-virgin olive oil for 2 hours, then strain.

Rustic Greek pie

14-oz. box frozen spinach, thawed
1 large sheet store-bought, unbaked
  piecrust, thawed
3 cloves garlic, finely chopped
5 oz. haloumi, grated
3/4 cup feta, crumbled
1 tablespoon fresh oregano sprigs
2 eggs
1/4 cup cream
lemon wedges, to serve

Preheat the oven to 400°F. Squeeze the excess liquid from the spinach.

Place the piecrust on a baking sheet and spread the spinach in the middle, leaving a 1 1/4-in. border around the edge. Sprinkle the garlic over the spinach and pile the haloumi and feta on top. Sprinkle with oregano and season well. Cut a short slit into each corner of the crust, then tuck each side of crust over to form a border around the filling.

Lightly beat the eggs with the cream and carefully pour the egg mixture over the spinach filling. Bake for 25–30 minutes or until the crust is golden and the filling is set. Serve with the lemon wedges and a fresh green salad.

Serves 4

Mushroom potpies

½ cup extra-virgin olive oil
1 leek, sliced
1 clove garlic, crushed
2 lbs. portobello mushrooms,
  roughly chopped
1 teaspoon chopped fresh thyme
1¼ cups whipping cream
1 sheet store-bought, unbaked puff
  pastry, thawed
1 egg yolk, beaten, to glaze

Preheat the oven to 350°F. Heat
1 tablespoon oil in a frying pan over
medium heat. Cook the leek and
garlic for 5 minutes or until the leek
is soft and translucent. Transfer to a
large saucepan.

Heat the remaining oil in the frying
pan over high heat and cook the
mushrooms in two batches, stirring
frequently, for 5–7 minutes per batch
or until the mushrooms have released
their juices and are soft. Transfer to
the saucepan, then add the thyme.

Place the saucepan over high heat
and stir in the cream until well mixed.
Cook, stirring occasionally, for
7–8 minutes or until the cream has
reduced to a thick sauce. Remove
from the heat and season well.

Divide the filling among four 1¼ cup
ramekins or flameproof bowls. Cut
the pastry into rounds slightly larger
than each dish. Brush the rim of
the ramekins with a little of the egg
yolk, place the pastry on top, and
press down to seal. Brush the top
with the remaining egg yolk. Place
the ramekins on a baking sheet. Bake
for 20–25 minutes or until the pastry
has risen and is golden brown. Great
with mashed potatoes and a salad.

Serves 4

Rack of lamb with mustard crust and parsley potatoes

2 racks of lamb (7–8 ribs each rack), trimmed
1/4 cup vegetable oil
2 cups fresh breadcrumbs
3 cloves garlic, chopped
1 teaspoon grated lemon zest
1/2 cup fresh Italian parsley, finely chopped
2 tablespoons tarragon Dijon mustard
2/3 cup unsalted butter, softened
3/4 lb. baby new potatoes

Preheat the oven to 425°F. Score the fat side of the racks in a crisscross pattern. Rub 1 tablespoon of the oil over the racks and season well. Heat the remaining oil in a frying pan over medium heat and cook the racks for 5–8 minutes or until the surface is completely brown. Remove from the pan.

Combine the breadcrumbs, garlic, lemon zest, and three quarters of the parsley. Add the mustard and 1/3 cup of the butter to form a paste. Firmly press a layer of breadcrumb mixture over the fat side of the racks, then place in a roasting pan. Bake for 25 minutes or until the breadcrumbs appear brown and crisp and the meat is cooked to medium. For well-done, continue to bake for 10 minutes or until cooked to your liking. Cover the breadcrumb crust with aluminum foil to keep it from burning, if necessary.

About 25 minutes before the lamb is ready, toss the potatoes with the remaining butter until well coated. Season, then put in a roasting pan. Bake for 20 minutes or until brown, then remove, sprinkle with the remaining parsley, and season. To serve, cut the racks in half using the bones as a guide. Serve with the pan juices, potatoes, and a tossed salad.

Serves 4

Roasted vegetable cannelloni

1/4 cup butter
1 large leek, cut into 1/2-in. pieces
7 oz. roasted eggplant in oil, from deli
7 oz. roasted orange sweet potato in oil, from deli
1 cup firmly packed grated cheddar
1/3 cup all-purpose flour
4 cups milk
6 fresh lasagna sheets

Preheat the oven to 400°F and lightly grease a ceramic dish (11 x 7 x 2 in.). Melt 1 tablespoon butter in a saucepan, add the leek, and stir over medium heat for 8 minutes or until soft. Chop the eggplant and sweet potato into 1/2-in. pieces and place in a bowl. Mix in the leek and 1/3 cup of the cheddar.

Melt the remaining butter in a saucepan over medium heat. Stir in the flour and cook for 1 minute or until foaming. Remove from the heat and gradually stir in the milk. Return to the heat and stir until the sauce boils and thickens. Reduce the heat and simmer for 2 minutes. Season with salt and ground black pepper. Stir 1 1/2 cups of the sauce into the vegetable mixture, adding extra if necessary to bind it together.

Cut the rectangular lasagna sheets in half widthwise to make two smaller rectangles. Spoon vegetable mixture along the center of one sheet and roll up. Repeat to make twelve tubes.

Place the tubes, seam-side down, in the dish and spoon the remaining white sauce over the top until they are covered. Sprinkle with the remaining cheese and bake for 20 minutes or until the cheese is golden.

Serves 4

Chili con carne

1 tablespoon vegetable oil
1 large red onion, finely chopped
2 cloves garlic, crushed
1½ teaspoons chili powder
1 teaspoon ground oregano
2 teaspoons ground cumin
1 lb. lean ground beef
2 14-oz. cans diced tomatoes
14-oz. can red kidney beans, drained
  and rinsed
8 flour tortillas
sour cream, to serve, optional

Preheat the oven to 350°F. Heat the oil in a large saucepan, add the onion and garlic, and cook, stirring, over medium heat for about 2–3 minutes or until softened. Add the chili powder, oregano, and cumin and stir until fragrant. Add the ground beef and cook, stirring, for about 5 minutes or until browned all over, breaking up any lumps with the back of a wooden spoon.

Add the tomatoes, beans, and ½ cup water and simmer, stirring occasionally, for 30 minutes or until thick. Season to taste with salt and pepper. Ten minutes before serving, wrap the tortillas in aluminum foil and heat them in the oven according to package instructions to soften. Fill the tortillas with the chili and wrap. Serve with sour cream and a green salad.

Serves 4

Note: You can top potatoes with chili con carne and a dollop of sour cream, or serve it with rice.

Chicken casserole with mustard and tarragon

1/4 cup extra-virgin olive oil
2 lbs. boneless chicken thighs,
   halved, then quartered
1 onion, finely chopped
1 leek, sliced
1 clove garlic, finely chopped
11 oz. button mushrooms, sliced
1/2 teaspoon dried tarragon
1 1/2 cups chicken stock
3/4 cup whipping cream
2 teaspoons lemon juice
2 teaspoons Dijon mustard

Preheat the oven to 350°F. Heat 1 tablespoon of the oil in a flameproof casserole dish over medium heat, and cook the chicken in two batches for 6–7 minutes each or until golden. Remove from the dish.

Add the remaining oil to the casserole and cook the onion, leek, and garlic over medium heat for 5 minutes or until soft. Add the mushrooms and cook for 5–7 minutes or until they are soft and browned and most of the liquid has evaporated. Add the tarragon, chicken stock, cream, lemon juice, and mustard, bring to a boil, and cook for 2 minutes. Return the chicken pieces to the casserole dish and season well. Cover.

Place the casserole dish in the oven and cook for 1 hour or until the sauce has reduced and thickened. Season to taste with salt and pepper and serve with potatoes and a green salad.

Serves 4–6

Pork crown roast with fig and Marsala sauce

3/4 lb. dessert figs, quartered
1/3 cup marsala
2 teaspoons Dijon mustard
1/2 cup chicken stock
3-lb. pork crown roast, tied
1/2 cup vegetable oil
1 large red onion, sliced
18 fresh sage leaves
2 1/2 cups beans, trimmed

Preheat the oven to 475°F. Soak the figs, marsala, mustard, and stock for 30 minutes. Score the rind of the pork in lines 2 inches apart, brush with 2 tablespoons oil, and season. Place in a large roasting pan, cook for 15 minutes, then reduce the heat to 400°F. Add the onion, bake for 40 minutes, then add the fig mixture and bake for 30–40 minutes or until the pork juices run clear when the thickest section is pierced with a skewer.

Meanwhile, heat the remaining oil in a small saucepan over high heat. Add the sage leaves a few at a time for 30 seconds per batch. Remove with a slotted spoon and drain.

Remove the pork and onion pieces from the oven and allow the meat to rest for 5 minutes. Drain the excess fat from the roasting pan. Reduce the sauce on the stovetop for 5 minutes, stirring to scrape up any sediment stuck to the bottom of the pan.

Cook the beans in boiling water for 4 minutes. Drain. Season.

Slice the pork into portions, pour on the sauce, and garnish with the sage leaves. Serve with the onions, beans, and mashed potatoes.

Serves 4

Squash tarts

6 sheets store-bought, unbaked
   puff pastry
2¼ lbs. butternut squash, cut into
   2½-in. pieces
6 tablespoons sour cream or cream
   cheese
sweet chili sauce, to serve

Preheat the oven to 400°F. Lightly grease six 4-in. tart dishes. Cut six 6-in. circles from the pastry, carefully place in the prepared dishes, and pleat the pastry to fit. Prick the pastry with a fork. Place on a baking sheet and bake for 15–20 minutes or until lightly golden, pressing down any pastry that puffs up. Allow to cool.

Meanwhile, steam the squash pieces for 15 minutes or until just tender.

Place a tablespoon of sour cream in the middle of each pastry shell and pile the pumpkin pieces on top. Season with salt and black pepper and drizzle with sweet chili sauce to taste. Return to the oven for 5 minutes to heat through. Remove from the pans and serve immediately.

Serves 6

Aromatic snapper packages

1 cup loosely packed fresh basil
  leaves, chopped
2 large cloves garlic, chopped
1 tablespoon lemon juice
1 teaspoon grated lemon zest
¼ cup extra-virgin olive oil
4 snapper fillets, trimmed, with
  skin and bones removed
  (about 6 oz. each)
1 lb. small new potatoes
20 asparagus spears
12 yellow baby squash

Preheat the oven to 400°F. Combine the basil, garlic, lemon juice, zest, and 2 tablespoons of the olive oil. Season.

Place a fish fillet in the center of a sheet of aluminum foil large enough to fully enclose it. Season. Smear the fillet with 2 teaspoons of the basil mixture, then wrap into a secure package with the foil. Repeat with the remaining fillets. Place on a baking sheet and refrigerate until needed.

Cook the potatoes in a saucepan of boiling water for 15–20 minutes or until tender. Drain and keep warm. While the potatoes are cooking, brush the asparagus and squash with the remaining oil. Place on a baking tray and season with freshly ground black pepper. Bake for 8–10 minutes or until golden and tender.

Ten minutes before the vegetables are ready, place the fish packages in the oven and cook for 5–7 minutes or until the flesh flakes easily when tested with a fork. Check one of the packages after 5 minutes to see if the fish is cooked through. Place the opened packages on serving plates with the vegetables, season to taste, and serve.

Serves 4

Mustard-crusted rib-eye steak with roasted vegetables

16 shallots
1/2 cup whole-grain mustard
3 cloves garlic, crushed
2 1/4–3 lbs. rib-eye steak
1/2 lb. parsnips, cut into 3/4-in. chunks
3/4 lb. potatoes, cut lengthwise
  into wedges
1/2 lb. orange sweet potato, cut
  into wedges
1/3 cup extra-virgin olive oil

Preheat the oven to 400°F. Peel four of the shallots, slice into thick rings, and arrange them in the center of a large roasting pan.

Combine the mustard and garlic and season well with salt and pepper. Rub the mixture over the surface of the beef, then place the beef on top of the sliced shallots. Toss the parsnips, potatoes, sweet potatoes, the remaining shallots, and 1/4 cup of the oil together, then arrange around the beef. Drizzle the remaining oil over the beef and roast for 30 minutes.

Season and turn the vegetables— don't worry if some of the mustard mixes through. Roast for another 30 minutes for medium-rare or until cooked to your liking. Rest in a warm place for 10 minutes.

To serve, carve the beef and spoon the pan juices on the top. Serve with the roasted vegetables and whole shallots.

Serves 4

Moroccan roast lamb with mint couscous

2 tablespoons extra-virgin olive oil
3 teaspoons ground cumin
3 teaspoons ground cilantro
3 teaspoons sweet paprika
3 cloves garlic, crushed
3-lb. boneless leg of lamb
1⅓ cups couscous
2 tablespoons chopped fresh mint

Preheat the oven to 350°F. Combine the oil, spices, and 2 cloves crushed garlic to form a smooth paste. Season with salt and pepper. Rub a thick coating of the paste all over the lamb. Place on a rack in a roasting pan and roast for 1 hour 15 minutes, basting two or three times. Allow to rest in a warm place for 10 minutes.

Meanwhile, place the couscous in a heatproof bowl with 2 cups boiling water. Stir in the mint, the remaining garlic, and ½ teaspoon salt. Cover and leave for 5 minutes or until all the water has been absorbed, then gently fluff with a fork.

To serve, carve the lamb into thick slices and place on a bed of couscous. Pour the pan juices into a small pitcher and serve with the lamb. Garnish with fresh mint leaves, if desired.

Serves 4

Note: The lamb is baked for a long time, but the rest of this recipe is easy and quick to prepare.

Baked ricotta with ratatouille

3 lbs. ricotta, well drained
4 eggs, lightly beaten
3 cloves garlic, finely chopped
2 tablespoons chopped fresh thyme
1/3 cup extra-virgin olive oil
3/4 lb. eggplant, diced
3 peppers, green, red, and yellow, diced
14-oz. can crushed tomatoes

Preheat the oven to 350°F. Place the ricotta, eggs, 1 finely chopped garlic clove, and 1 tablespoon chopped fresh thyme in a bowl. Season and mix well. Pour the mixture into a lightly greased 9-in. springform pan and gently tap a couple of times to expel any air bubbles. Bake for 1 1/2 hours or until firm and golden. Cool on a rack, pressing down from time to time to remove any air bubbles.

Meanwhile, heat 2 tablespoons oil in a frying pan, add the eggplant, and cook for 4–5 minutes or until golden. Add the peppers and remaining garlic and cook for 5 minutes, adding an extra tablespoon of oil if necessary. Stir in the tomatoes and remaining thyme and cook for 10–15 minutes or until rich and pulpy. Season. Remove the ricotta from the springform pan and cut into wedges. Serve with a little ratatouille on the side, garnished with thyme sprigs.

Serves 8

Note: Although this recipe cooks for a long time, it is quick to prepare.

Balsamic roasted veal cutlets with red onion

1 ½ tablespoons extra-virgin olive oil
8 veal cutlets
4 cloves garlic, unpeeled
1 red onion, cut into thin wedges
1 tablespoon chopped fresh rosemary
½ lb. cherry tomatoes
¼ cup balsamic vinegar
2 teaspoons light brown sugar
2 tablespoons chopped fresh
   Italian parsley

Preheat the oven to 400°F. Heat the oil in a large frying pan over medium heat. Cook the cutlets in batches for 4 minutes on both sides or until brown.

Arrange the cutlets in a single layer in a large, shallow-sided roasting pan. Add the garlic, onion, rosemary, tomatoes, vinegar, and sugar. Season well with salt and freshly ground black pepper.

Cover tightly with aluminum foil and roast for 15 minutes. Remove the foil and roast for another 10–15 minutes, depending on the thickness of the veal.

Transfer the cutlets, garlic, onion, and tomatoes to serving plates. Stir the pan juices and spoon over the top. Garnish with the chopped parsley and serve immediately. Delicious with creamy garlic mashed potatoes and a tossed green salad.

Serves 4

Chicken, broccoli, and pasta bake

10 oz. fusilli
14-oz. can cream of mushroom soup
2 eggs
3/4 cup mayonnaise
1 tablespoon Dijon mustard
1 2/3 cups grated cheddar
1 1/4 lbs. boneless chicken breasts,
   thinly sliced
13 oz. frozen broccoli pieces, thawed
1/2 cup fresh breadcrumbs

Preheat the oven to 350°F. Cook the pasta in a large saucepan of boiling water until al dente, then drain and return to the pan. Combine the soup, eggs, mayonnaise, mustard, and half the cheese in a bowl.

Heat a lightly greased nonstick frying pan over medium heat, add the chicken slices, and cook for 5–6 minutes or until cooked through. Season with salt and pepper, then set aside to cool.

Add the chicken and broccoli to the pasta, pour the soup mixture over the top, and stir until well combined. Transfer the mixture to a 12-cup, flameproof dish. Sprinkle with the combined breadcrumbs and remaining cheese. Bake for 20 minutes or until the top is golden brown.

Serves 6–8

Roast peppered steak with onions and potatoes

2 lbs. New York strip steak
2 tablespoons freshly ground black
  peppercorns
1 large red onion
4 large potatoes
1/4 cup butter
1/4 cup beef stock
1/4 cup red wine
1 lb. mixed yellow and green beans

Preheat the oven to 350°F. Trim the excess fat from the steak, leaving a thin layer. Press the pepper all over the steak.

Cut the onion and potatoes into 1/4-in.-thick slices and place in a roasting pan. Sit the steak on top, fat-side up. Cut 2 tablespoons of the butter into small pieces and dot all over the steak and potatoes. Pour in the stock and wine and bake for 35–40 minutes for medium-rare or until cooked to your liking. Remove the steak from the oven and rest for at least 5 minutes before carving.

Meanwhile, bring a saucepan of lightly salted water to a boil. Add the mixed beans and cook for 2–4 minutes or until just tender. Drain well, then add the remaining butter and toss. Keep warm until ready to serve.

To serve, divide the onion and potato mixture among four serving plates and top with slices of steak. Spoon on any pan juices and serve with the beans.

Serves 4

Shepherd's pie with garlic mashed potatoes

1½ tablespoons vegetable oil
1 large onion, finely chopped
1 carrot, finely diced
8 garlic cloves, peeled
1½ lbs. lean ground lamb
1½ cups tomato pasta sauce
1¼ cups beef stock
1¾ lbs. potatoes, cut into
    large chunks
1½ tablespoons butter

Heat the oil in a large saucepan over medium heat. Cook the onion and carrot for 5 minutes or until soft. Crush 2 garlic cloves and sauté with the onion for another minute. Add the ground lamb and stir well, breaking up any lumps with a wooden spoon. Cook for 5 minutes or until browned and cooked through. Spoon off any excess fat, then add the pasta sauce and 1 cup stock. Cover and bring to a boil. Reduce the heat to medium-low and simmer for 25 minutes. Uncover and cook for 20 minutes or until the sauce thickens. Preheat the oven to 400°F.

Meanwhile, cook the potatoes in a saucepan of boiling water with the remaining garlic for 15–20 minutes or until tender. Drain well, then return to the saucepan over low heat, stirring to evaporate any excess water. Remove from the heat, add the butter and the remaining stock, and mash until smooth. Season.

Transfer the lamb mixture to a 6-cup, flameproof, ceramic dish. Spread the potatoes over the top. Use a fork to swirl the surface. Bake for 40 minutes or until golden brown.

Serves 4

Note: Shepherd's pie has a long cooking time but is quick to prepare.

Artichoke, olive, and goat cheese pizza

10-in. store-bought pizza base
1/3 cup store-bought pasta sauce
2/3 cup marinated artichokes,
  quartered
1/2 cup pitted Kalamata olives
1 clove garlic, thinly sliced
2 oz. goat cheese, crumbled
extra-virgin olive oil, to drizzle
2 tablespoons chopped fresh oregano

Preheat the oven to 425°F. Place the pizza base on a baking sheet, then spread with the pasta sauce. Evenly sprinkle the artichoke pieces, olives, and garlic over the pasta sauce, then top with the crumbled goat cheese.

Lightly drizzle the surface of the pizza with olive oil and bake for 20 minutes or until golden. Sprinkle with fresh oregano and season with salt and freshly ground black pepper. Cut into wedges and serve.

Serves 4

Lamb kofta curry

1¼ cups jasmine rice
2 lbs. lean ground lamb
1 egg, lightly beaten
2 onions, finely chopped
4-oz. jar Korma curry paste
4 tablespoons chopped cilantro
  leaves
2 cloves garlic, crushed
2 tablespoons vegetable oil
14-oz. can diced tomatoes

Preheat the oven to 425°F and lightly grease two baking sheets. Bring a large saucepan of water to a boil. Add the rice and cook for 12 minutes, stirring occasionally. Drain.

Meanwhile, combine the ground lamb, egg, 1 onion, 2 tablespoons curry paste, 3 tablespoons cilantro, 1 garlic clove, and salt, and form tablespoons of the mixture into balls. Place on one of the baking sheets.

Heat 1 tablespoon oil in a large nonstick frying pan over medium heat. Cook the balls in batches for 1 minute on each side or until evenly golden, but not cooked through. Place on the second sheet and bake for 5–7 minutes or until cooked through.

Wipe the pan clean. Heat the remaining oil over medium heat. Add the remaining onion and garlic and cook for 3 minutes or until the onion is soft. Add the remaining curry paste, cook for 1 minute, then add the tomatoes and 1 cup water. Bring to a boil, then reduce the heat and simmer for 10 minutes or until the sauce thickens slightly. Season. Stir the meatballs and their juices into the sauce. Simmer for 5 minutes to warm the meatballs. Serve with rice and sprinkle with cilantro.

Serves 4

Mexican chicken bake

3/4 cup short-grain rice
1 1/2 cups canned red kidney beans,
  drained and thoroughly rinsed
3 1/2 tablespoons chopped cilantro
  leaves
1 tablespoon vegetable oil
1 1/4 lbs. skinless, boneless chicken
  thighs
12-oz. jar spicy taco sauce
2 cups grated cheddar
1/2 cup sour cream

Preheat the oven to 350°F. Lightly grease a deep, round, 8 1/2-in. ceramic casserole dish. Bring a large saucepan of water to a boil, add the rice, and cook for 10–12 minutes, stirring occasionally. Drain.

In the prepared dish, combine the beans and 1 1/2 tablespoons of the cilantro, then add the rice and toss together. Lightly press the mixture so that the beans are mixed into the rice and the mixture is flat.

Heat the oil in a large frying pan over medium-high heat. Sauté the chicken thighs for 3 minutes, then turn over. Add the spicy taco sauce and cook for another 3 minutes.

To assemble, spread half the cheese over the rice. Arrange the thighs and sauce on top in a star shape, sprinkle with 1 1/2 tablespoons cilantro, then sprinkle with cheese. Cover with aluminum foil.

Bake for 35–40 minutes or until the mixture is bubbling and the cheese is melted and slightly browned—remove the foil for the last 5 minutes. Cut into four servings with a knife and scoop out carefully, keeping the layers intact. Serve sprinkled with the remaining cilantro and a dollop of sour cream.

Serves 4

Pork loin roast with apple walnut stuffing and roast vegetables

1/2 cup walnuts, chopped
1 green apple, peeled and cored
1/2 teaspoon ground cinnamon
2 tablespoons port
3 lbs. rindless, boneless pork loin
1/2 cup maple syrup
8 parsnips, sliced thinly lengthwise
1 lb. baby carrots
2 tablespoons vegetable oil

Preheat the oven to 400°F. Grease a large roasting pan. Spread the walnuts on a baking sheet and place under a medium-high broiler for 2–3 minutes or until lightly toasted.

Coarsely grate the apple and squeeze out the excess juice. Combine the apple, cinnamon, walnuts, and port and season to taste.

Unroll the pork loin, then spread the stuffing evenly over one-third of the loin lengthwise. Reroll the loin, tie securely, and place, seam-side down, in the prepared pan. Roast for 20 minutes. Reduce the heat to 350°F, baste the pork with some maple syrup, and roast for another 30 minutes.

Toss together the parsnips, carrots, and oil in a large bowl and season if necessary. Add to the roasting pan and roast for another 30–35 minutes or until the vegetables are golden and tender. In the last 10 minutes of cooking, baste the pork again with the syrup. Remove the roast pork from the pan, cover with aluminum foil, and allow to rest for 10 minutes before slicing. Serve with the vegetables and any pan juices.

Serves 4

John Dory fillets in a spicy tomato sauce

4 John Dory fillets (or other firm white fish), 1 in. thick, about ½ lb. each
1¼ cups long-grain rice
2 tablespoons vegetable oil
1 teaspoon coriander seeds, lightly crushed
1 teaspoon black mustard seeds
1½ tablespoons sambal oelek
14-oz. can diced tomatoes
1 teaspoon garam masala
10-oz. bag baby spinach leaves

Preheat the oven to 350°F. Pat the fillets dry with paper towels. Bring a large saucepan of water to a boil. Add the rice and cook for 12 minutes, stirring occasionally. Drain well.

Meanwhile, heat 1 tablespoon of the oil in a saucepan over medium heat. When hot, add the coriander and mustard seeds—the mustard seeds should start to pop after 30 seconds. Add the sambal oelek and cook for 30 seconds, then stir in the tomatoes and the garam masala. Bring to a boil, then reduce the heat to low and simmer, covered, for 6–8 minutes or until the sauce thickens.

Heat the remaining oil in a large nonstick frying pan over medium heat. Add the fillets and cook for 1 minute each side or until evenly browned but not cooked through. Transfer to an 11 x 7-in. ceramic baking dish. Spoon the tomato sauce over the fillets and bake for 10 minutes or until the fish is cooked through.

Meanwhile, wash the spinach and put in a saucepan with just the water clinging to the leaves. Cook, covered, for 1 minute or until wilted. Serve the fish fillets topped with sauce, with the spinach and the rice.

Serves 4

Herbed garlic mushrooms with goat cheese bruschetta

1/3 cup butter
4 cloves garlic, crushed
2/3 cup chopped fresh Italian parsley
4 large portobello mushrooms,
   3–4 oz. each, stems removed
4 large slices Italian bread, sliced
   diagonally
2 tablespoons extra-virgin olive oil
5 oz. goat cheese, at room
   temperature
2 cups baby arugula leaves

Preheat the oven to 350°F. Melt the butter in a small saucepan, add the garlic and parsley, and cook, stirring, for 1 minute or until well combined. Spoon the mixture evenly over the underside of the mushrooms. Line a baking sheet with waxed paper. Place the mushrooms on the baking sheet, filling-side up, and cover with aluminum foil. Bake for 20 minutes or until softened and cooked through.

Toward the end of the cooking time, brush both sides of the bread with the olive oil and grill or broil until crisp and golden on both sides.

Spread the bruschetta with the soft goat cheese and top with the arugula. Cut the hot garlic mushrooms in half and place two halves on each bruschetta, then drizzle with the cooking juices and season with ground black pepper. Serve immediately to keep the bread from getting soggy.

Serves 4

Roasted lamb shanks in rich tomato sauce on polenta

2 tablespoons extra-virgin olive oil
1 large red onion, sliced
4 French-trimmed lamb shanks
(about 1/2 lb. each)
2 cloves garlic, crushed
14-oz. can diced tomatoes
1/2 cup red wine
2 teaspoons chopped fresh rosemary
1 cup instant polenta
1/4 cup butter
1/2 cup grated Parmesan

Preheat the oven to 315°F. Heat the oil in a 16-cup flameproof casserole dish over medium heat and sauté the onion for 3–4 minutes or until softened and becoming transparent. Add the lamb shanks and cook for 2–3 minutes or until lightly browned. Add the garlic, tomatoes, and wine, then bring to a boil and cook for 3–4 minutes. Stir in the rosemary. Season with 1/4 teaspoon each of salt and pepper.

Cover and bake for 2 hours. Uncover, return to the oven, and simmer for another 15 minutes or until the lamb just starts to fall off the bone. Check periodically that the sauce is not too dry, adding water if needed.

Twenty minutes before serving, bring 4 cups of water to a boil in a saucepan. Add the polenta in a thin stream, whisking continuously, then reduce the heat to very low. Simmer for 8–10 minutes or until thick and coming away from the side of the saucepan. Stir in the butter and Parmesan. To serve, spoon the polenta onto serving plates and top with the shanks and a little sauce from the casserole over the shanks.

Serves 4

Note: Although this dish has a long cooking time, the preparation is fast.

Baked Mediterranean pork chops

4 large pork loin chops, trimmed
2 tablespoons extra-virgin olive oil
2 cloves garlic, finely chopped
1 tablespoon finely chopped fresh
  rosemary
2 tablespoons fresh thyme
2 tablespoons balsamic vinegar
4 Roma tomatoes, halved lengthwise
1 large red pepper, cut into 3/4-in.
  strips
4 small zucchini, trimmed and
  halved lengthwise

Preheat the oven to 425°F and lightly grease a baking pan. Arrange the pork chops in a single layer in the pan. Combine the olive oil, garlic, rosemary, thyme, and 1 tablespoon of the balsamic vinegar, then spoon half the mixture over the pork chops. Season to taste with salt and black pepper. Cover with plastic wrap and marinate for 20 minutes.

Place 2 tomato halves, cut-side down, on each pork chop and sprinkle the tomatoes with the remaining balsamic vinegar.

Toss the pepper and zucchini with the remaining herb mixture, then add to the dish around the chops. Bake for 45 minutes or until cooked through and well browned. Season to taste. Serve the chops with the roast vegetables, a green salad, and bread.

Serves 4

Baked potatoes with avocado, tomato, and corn salsa

4 large potatoes
2 vine-ripened tomatoes, seeded
  and chopped
1/2 cup corn, drained
2 scallions, chopped
1 tablespoon lime juice
1/2 teaspoon sugar
1 avocado, diced
1/4 cup chopped cilantro leaves
1 tablespoon sour cream, optional

Preheat the oven to 415°F. Pierce the potatoes all over with a fork. Bake directly on the oven rack for 1 hour or until tender when tested with a skewer. Leave for 2 minutes. Cut a cross in the top of each potato and squeeze gently from the bottom to open (if the potatoes are still too hot, hold them in a clean dishcloth).

While the potatoes are cooking, put the tomatoes, corn, scallions, lime juice, and sugar in a bowl and mix well. Add the avocado and cilantro leaves. Season. Spoon some mixture onto each potato and, if desired, add a dollop of sour cream.

Serves 4

Note: You can also make a chicken topping. Cook two chicken breasts in 2 cups boiling chicken stock for 5 minutes. Remove from the heat and cool in the liquid. Shred the meat. Add 2 tablespoons mayonnaise, 1 teaspoon grated lemon zest, and 1 tablespoon baby capers. Toss 3 cups shredded arugula with 1 tablespoon extra-virgin olive oil, 1 tablespoon balsamic vinegar, and 1 sliced avocado. Place some onto each potato and top with the chicken mixture. Season to taste.

Tortilla pie

1 tablespoon vegetable oil
1 lb. lean ground beef
1/4-oz. package taco seasoning mix
14-oz. can chili beans, drained
8 flour tortillas
2 cups grated cheddar
10-oz. jar salsa
2/3 cup sour cream
1 avocado, diced

Preheat the oven to 350°F. Grease a 9-in. pie dish. Heat the oil in a large nonstick frying pan. Add the ground beef and cook for 5 minutes or until brown, breaking up the lumps with the back of a spoon. Drain off the excess oil. Add the seasoning mix and cook for 5 minutes. Stir in the beans until heated through.

Lay a tortilla in the bottom of the pie dish, then spread 1/2 cup of the beef mixture on top. Sprinkle with 1/4 cup cheese and 1 tablespoon salsa. Continue layering with the remaining tortillas, beef mixture, cheese, and salsa, ending with a tortilla sprinkled with a little cheese—it should end up looking like a dome shape.

Bake for 15 minutes or until all the cheese has melted and browned. Cool slightly, cut into wedges, and top with a dollop of sour cream and the diced avocado. Serve with a salad.

Serves 4

Ham and cheese pasta bake

1½ tablespoons extra-virgin olive oil
1 onion, finely chopped
10-oz. ham, sliced ⅛ in. thick
   and cut into 2-in. pieces
2½ cups whipping cream
2 cups cooked fresh peas or frozen
   peas, thawed
¾ lb. conchiglione (pasta shells)
3 tablespoons roughly chopped .
   fresh basil
2 cups grated mature cheddar

Preheat the oven to 400°F and lightly grease a 10-cup flameproof ceramic dish. Heat 1 tablespoon of the oil in a frying pan over medium heat and cook the onion, stirring frequently for 5 minutes or until soft. Add the remaining oil and the ham and cook, stirring, for 1 minute. Pour the cream into the pan, bring to a boil, then reduce the heat and simmer for 6 minutes. Add the peas and cook for another 2–4 minutes or until the mixture has reduced and thickened slightly. Season with freshly ground black pepper.

Meanwhile, cook the pasta in a large saucepan of rapidly boiling salted water according to the package instructions until al dente. Drain and return to the saucepan.

Add the cream sauce to the pasta, then add the basil and three-quarters of the cheese. Stir well and season. Transfer the mixture to the prepared dish, sprinkle on the remaining cheese, and bake for 20 minutes or until the top is golden brown.

Serves 4

Note: Other pasta shapes, such as spirals, farfalle, fusilli, or macaroni, can be used for this dish.

Thai ginger fish with cilantro butter

1/4 cup butter, at room temperature
1 tablespoon finely chopped
    cilantro leaves
2 tablespoons lime juice
1 tablespoon vegetable oil
1 tablespoon grated palm sugar or
    brown sugar
4 fresh long red chilies, seeded
    and chopped
2 lemongrass stalks, trimmed
4 firm white fish fillets (blue eye
    or John Dory), about 6 oz. each
1 lime, thinly sliced
1 tablespoon finely shredded
    fresh ginger

Thoroughly mix the butter and cilantro and roll it into a log. Wrap the log in plastic wrap and chill in the refrigerator until needed.

Preheat the oven to 400°F. Combine the lime juice, oil, sugar, and chilies in a small, nonmetallic bowl and stir until the sugar has dissolved. Cut the lemongrass into halves.

Place a piece of lemongrass in the center of a sheet of aluminum foil large enough to fully enclose one fillet. Place a fish fillet on top and smear the surface with the lime juice mixture. Top with some lime slices and ginger shreds, then wrap into a secure package. Repeat with the remaining ingredients to make four packages.

Place the packages in a flameproof dish and bake for 8–10 minutes or until the fish flakes easily when tested with a fork.

To serve, place the packages on individual serving plates and serve open with slices of cilantro butter, steamed rice, and steamed greens.

Serves 4

Sausage and bean stew with roasted orange sweet potatoes

2 lbs. spicy, Italian-style sausages
2 cloves garlic, roughly chopped
2 14-oz. cans cannellini beans
2 14-oz. cans crushed tomatoes
2 teaspoons Dijon mustard
1 1/2 lbs. orange sweet potatoes, cut into 1 1/4-in. cubes
2 tablespoons extra-virgin olive oil
2 tablespoons coarsely chopped Italian parsley

Preheat the oven to 400°F. Cook the sausages in a large frying pan over medium heat for 5–7 minutes or until golden. Cut into 2-in. pieces and place in a 16-cup casserole dish. Add the garlic, beans, tomatoes, mustard, and 2 tablespoons water to the dish and season with pepper. Stir well and cover with a lid. Place in the oven.

Meanwhile, toss the sweet potatoes with the oil and place in a baking dish. Sprinkle with salt. Place in the oven with the casserole dish and bake for 25 minutes. Uncover the casserole dish and bake for another 10–15 minutes or until the stew is golden and bubbling and the sweet potatoes are soft and lightly golden brown. Serve the stew garnished with the parsley and the sweet potatoes on the side.

Serves 4

Vegetable bake

3/4 lb. potatoes, thinly sliced
lengthwise
1/4 cup butter, melted
1 1/2–2 teaspoons finely chopped fresh
thyme
3/4 lb. squash, thinly sliced
4 cups zucchini, thinly sliced
lengthwise
1 cup tomato pasta sauce
1/2 cup grated Parmesan

Preheat the oven to 325°F. Grease a 6-cup, rectangular, flameproof dish. Combine the potatoes with one-third each of the butter and thyme. Season, then place in the bottom of the prepared dish.

Combine the squash and another third of the butter and thyme. Season to taste and press onto the potatoes. Combine the zucchini with the remaining butter and thyme. Season and press onto the squash.

Spread the pasta sauce evenly over the top and cover with greased aluminum foil. Bake for 45 minutes, remove the foil, and sprinkle with the grated Parmesan. Bake for another 15 minutes or until the top is golden brown and the vegetables are cooked through. Serve with a salad and bread.

Serves 4

Chicken and leek pies

¼ cup butter
1 leek, thinly sliced
4 6-oz. chicken breasts
½ cup all-purpose flour
1 cup chicken and herb stock
1¼ cups whipping cream
1 cup fresh or frozen peas, blanched
1 sheet store-bought puff pastry,
  thawed

Melt the butter in a saucepan over medium heat and cook the leek for 2–3 minutes or until soft. Add the chicken and cook for 45 minutes or until done. Add the flour and cook, stirring, until it starts to bubble. Add the stock and cook until the mixture starts to thicken. Add the cream, reserving 1 tablespoon to glaze the pastry. Cook until the mixture just starts to boil. Stir in the peas. Season. Remove from the heat. Preheat the oven to 400°F.

Divide the filling among four individual pie dishes or ramekins. Top with a round of pastry, cut just bigger than the top of the dish, then press around the edges to seal. Brush the surface with the reserved cream. Make a small slit in the top to allow steam to escape. Place the dishes on a baking sheet and bake for 20–25 minutes or until the pastry is golden. Serve with a green salad.

Serves 4

Dessert

Strawberries with balsamic vinegar

1½ lbs. ripe small strawberries
¼ cup sugar
2 tablespoons balsamic vinegar
½ cup mascarpone

Wipe the strawberries with a clean, damp cloth and carefully remove the green stems. If the strawberries are large, cut each one in half.

Place all the strawberries in a large glass bowl, sprinkle the sugar evenly over the top, and toss gently to coat. Set aside for 2 hours to macerate, then sprinkle the balsamic vinegar over the strawberries. Toss them again, then refrigerate for 30 minutes.

Spoon the strawberries into four glasses, drizzle with the liquid, and top with a dollop of mascarpone.

Serves 4

Note: Refrigerate the strawberries if you plan to macerate for longer than 2 hours.

Panna cotta with passion fruit sauce

extra-virgin olive oil, for brushing
2½ teaspoons powdered gelatin
1¼ cups goat's milk or regular milk
1¼ cups whipping cream
2 tablespoons sugar
1 teaspoon vanilla extract

Passion fruit sauce
3 tablespoons sugar
⅓ cup fresh passion fruit pulp

Lightly brush four ½-cup molds or ramekins with light olive oil. Place the gelatin and 2 tablespoons water in a small bowl. Place over a bowl of hot water and stir until dissolved.

Put the milk, cream, and sugar in a small saucepan. Gently heat to just under the boiling point, stirring so all the sugar dissolves. Remove from the heat and whisk in the gelatin mixture until dissolved. Allow to cool for a few minutes, then stir in the vanilla extract. Pour into the molds and refrigerate for 6 hours or until set.

Meanwhile, to make the passion fruit sauce, place the sugar and ½ cup water in a small saucepan over medium heat and stir for 3 minutes or until the sugar has dissolved. Remove from the heat and stir in the passion fruit pulp. Pour into a small pitcher and refrigerate until needed. Lightly run a knife around the side of each mold and unmold onto serving plates. Spoon the passion fruit sauce over the top and serve chilled.

Serves 4

Note: Although these require 6 hours refrigeration, they are quick to prepare.

Flourless chocolate cake

¹/₂ cup light brown sugar
6 eggs
13 oz. dark chocolate
1 tablespoon Grand Marnier
1 teaspoon ground cinnamon
1¹/₄ cups heavy whipping cream,
  plus extra, to serve
confectioners' sugar, to dust
strawberries, to serve

Preheat the oven to 350°F. Grease a 9-in. round cake pan and line the bottom with waxed paper. Beat the sugar and eggs in a bowl for 10 minutes or until creamy.

Meanwhile, chop the chocolate into small, evenly sized pieces and place in a heatproof bowl. Bring a saucepan of water to a boil, then remove from the heat. Allow the bowl to rest on the saucepan, making sure the bottom of the bowl does not touch the water. Stir occasionally until the chocolate has melted. Place the Grand Marnier, cinnamon, egg mixture, and melted chocolate in a bowl and mix together. Stir the cream very gently by hand 2–3 times and then fold into the chocolate mixture.

Pour the mixture into the prepared pan and bake for 1 hour or until a skewer comes out clean. Allow to cool in the pan, then unmold onto a wire rack when cool. Cut into slices, dust with confectioners' sugar, and serve with a dollop of cream and strawberries.

Serves 8

Note: This is a moist cake that will fall a little in the middle. If you prefer, use brandy, Tia Maria, or Cointreau instead of Grand Marnier.

Coconut lime ice cream

¹/₄ cup dried coconut
1 ¹/₂ tablespoons grated lime zest
¹/₃ cup lime juice
4 tablespoons coconut milk powder
4 cups vanilla ice cream, softened
coconut macaroon cookies, to serve

Combine the dried coconut, grated lime zest, lime juice, and coconut milk powder in a bowl and mix well.

Add the coconut mixture to the ice cream and fold through with a large metal spoon until evenly incorporated. Work quickly so that the ice cream does not melt. Return the mixture to the freezer for 30 minutes to firm. Serve with some coconut macaroon cookies on the side.

Serves 4

Apple galettes

¼ cup honey
pinch of pumpkin pie spice
2 large green apples
2 sheets prepared puff pastry
3 tablespoons ground almonds
2 teaspoons confectioners' sugar
2 tablespoons butter, cubed
heavy whipping cream, to serve

Preheat the oven to 415°F. Place the honey, pumpkin pie spice, and $2/3$ cup water in a saucepan and stir to combine. Peel, core, and thinly slice the apples. Add to the saucepan, cover, and cook over low heat for 8 minutes or until the apples are tender. Stir gently halfway through cooking. Cool and drain the apples, reserving the juice. Return the juice to the saucepan and boil for 10 minutes or until syrupy.

Cut the puff pastry into four 5-in. rounds, place on a lightly greased baking sheet, and sprinkle with the ground almonds. Arrange the apple slices over the pastry in a spiral pattern. Dust heavily with the confectioners' sugar and dot the butter over the apples. Bake for 15–20 minutes or until puffed and golden. Drizzle with the syrup and serve with cream.

Serves 4

Roasted pineapple gratin

1³/₄ lbs. ripe pineapple, cut into
  ¹/₂-in. cubes
¹/₄ cup dark rum
2 tablespoons unsalted butter
1 teaspoon vanilla extract
¹/₄ cup light brown sugar
¹/₂ teaspoon ground ginger
1¹/₄ cups sour cream
¹/₄ cup whipping cream
1 teaspoon finely grated lemon zest
¹/₂ cup light brown sugar, extra

Place the pineapple cubes, rum, butter, vanilla, sugar, and ginger in a large saucepan, and cook, stirring occasionally, for 8–10 minutes or until caramelized. Remove from the heat.

Divide the pineapple cubes among four individual gratin dishes and allow to cool slightly.

Combine the sour cream, cream, and lemon zest in a bowl, then spoon evenly over the pineapple cubes. Sprinkle the extra sugar over each gratin.

Cook the gratins under a hot broiler for 4–5 minutes or until the sugar has melted and caramelized. Be careful not to burn them. Serve immediately.

Serves 4

Poached pears in saffron citrus syrup

1 vanilla bean
1/2 teaspoon firmly packed saffron
   threads
3/4 cup sugar
2 teaspoons grated lemon zest
4 pears, peeled, stems attached
whipped cream, to serve, optional
biscotti, to serve, optional

Place the vanilla bean, saffron threads, sugar, and lemon zest in a saucepan with 4 cups water and mix well. Stir over low heat until the sugar dissolves. Bring to a boil, then reduce the heat and simmer for 10–12 minutes or until slightly reduced and syrupy.

Add the pears and cook, covered, for 12–15 minutes or until tender when tested with a metal skewer. Turn the pears over with a slotted spoon halfway through cooking. Once cooked, remove from the syrup.

Bring to a boil and cook for 10 minutes or until the syrup has reduced by half and thickened slightly. Remove the vanilla bean and serve the syrup drizzled over the pears with whipped cream and biscotti.

Serves 4

Tiramisu

18-oz. package yellow
  cake mix
3 eggs
1/3 cup vegetable oil
1 1/4 cups heavy whipping cream
1/4 cup confectioners' sugar
1 cup mascarpone, chilled
1/2 cup Kahlua
1 1/2 tablespoons instant coffee
  grounds
grated chocolate

Preheat the oven to 350°F. Grease a 9-in. square cake pan and line the bottom with waxed paper. Beat the cake mix, eggs, oil, and 1 1/4 cups water in a large bowl with an electric mixer on low speed for 30 seconds. Increase the speed and beat for 2 minutes or until well combined. Pour into the pan and bake for 35–40 minutes or until a skewer comes out clean when inserted into the center of the cake. Turn out onto a wire rack to cool. Beat the cream and sugar with a whisk until stiff. Fold in the mascarpone and 2 teaspoons of the Kahlua. Combine the coffee and the remaining Kahlua, stirring until the coffee has dissolved.

Cut the cake in half horizontally. Place the bottom of the cake on a serving plate and brush liberally with the coffee mixture, then spread a third of the cream mixture on top. Top with the other layer of cake and brush with the remaining coffee mixture. Spread the remaining cream mixture over the top and sides. Sprinkle the surface with grated chocolate to serve.

Serves 6–8

Figs with amaretto mascarpone

1/4 cup sugar
1/4 cup whipping cream
1/2 teaspoon vanilla extract
1/2 cup mascarpone
1/4 cup amaretto
1 1/2 tablespoons sugar, extra
1/4 cup blanched almonds,
  finely chopped
1/2 teaspoon ground cinnamon
6 fresh figs, halved

Line a baking sheet with aluminum foil. Place the sugar and 1/4 cup water in a small saucepan and stir over low heat until the sugar has dissolved, brushing down the side of the pan with a clean brush dipped in water if any crystals appear. Bring to a boil and cook, without stirring, for 8 minutes, swirling occasionally until the mixture is golden. Quickly remove the pan from the heat and carefully pour in the cream, stirring constantly until smooth, then stir in the vanilla extract.

To make the amaretto mascarpone, place the mascarpone, amaretto, and 2 teaspoons of the extra sugar in a bowl and mix together well.

Combine the almonds, cinnamon, and remaining sugar on a plate.

Press the cut side of each fig-half into the almond mixture, then place, cut-side up, onto the baking sheet. Cook under a hot broiler for 4–5 minutes or until the sugar has caramelized and the almonds are nicely toasted— watch carefully to prevent burning.

Arrange three fig halves on each plate, place a dollop of the amaretto mascarpone on the side, and drizzle with the sauce.

Serves 4

Mini coffee and walnut sour cream cakes

3/4 cup walnuts
2/3 cup firmly packed light brown
  sugar
1/2 cup unsalted butter, softened
2 eggs, lightly beaten
1 cup self-rising flour
1/3 cup sour cream
1 tablespoon coffee with
  chicory extract

Preheat the oven to 315°F. Lightly grease two 12-cup muffin pans. Process the walnuts and 1/4 cup of the brown sugar in a food processor until the walnuts are roughly chopped into small pieces. Transfer to a bowl.

Cream the butter and remaining sugar together in the food processor until pale and creamy. With the motor running, gradually add the eggs and process until smooth. Add the flour and blend until well mixed. Add the sour cream and coffee and process until thoroughly mixed.

Spoon half a teaspoon of the walnut and sugar mixture into the bottom of each muffin cup, followed by a teaspoon of the cake mixture. Sprinkle a little more walnut mixture over the top, then a little more cake mixture, and top with the remaining walnut mixture. Bake for 20 minutes or until risen and springy to the touch. Leave in the pans for 5 minutes. Remove the cakes using the handle of a teaspoon to loosen the side and bottom, then transfer to a wire rack to cool completely.

Makes 24

Individual self-saucing chocolate puddings

3/4 cup self-rising flour
1 tablespoon cocoa powder, plus
   3 teaspoons, extra
1/2 cup sugar
1 egg, lightly beaten
1/4 cup milk
1/4 cup butter, melted
1/3 cup light brown sugar
confectioners' sugar, to dust

Preheat the oven to 350°F. Lightly grease four 1/2-cup, flameproof dishes. Sift the flour and 1 tablespoon cocoa into a small bowl and add the sugar. Stir in the combined egg, milk, and butter and mix together well.

Spoon the mixture into the dishes and sprinkle with the combined sugar and extra cocoa powder. Place on a baking sheet and carefully pour 1/4 cup boiling water over the back of a metal spoon, for even coverage, over each pudding. Bake the puddings for 15–20 minutes or until a skewer comes out clean when inserted halfway in. Dust with confectioners' sugar, then serve immediately with whipped cream or ice cream.

Serves 4

Note: When testing to see whether the puddings are ready, insert your skewer at an angle. This way there is a larger area being checked.

Passion fruit bavarois

1½ cups passion fruit pulp
10 oz. silken tofu, chopped
2½ cups buttermilk
2 tablespoons sugar
1 teaspoon vanilla extract
6 teaspoons gelatin
¾ cup fresh passion fruit pulp, extra
½ lb. strawberries, halved

Push the passion fruit through a strainer. Discard the seeds, then place the syrup, tofu, buttermilk, sugar, and vanilla in a blender and blend for 90 seconds on high to mix thoroughly. Leave in the blender.

Place ⅓ cup water in a heatproof bowl and sprinkle the gelatin on top. Stand the bowl in a saucepan of very hot water and stir until the gelatin has dissolved and the mixture is smooth. Cool slightly.

Place eight ¾-cup dariol molds in a baking dish. Add the gelatin mixture to the blender and mix on high for 1 minute. Pour into the dariol molds, cover the dish with plastic wrap, and chill overnight.

When ready to serve, carefully run a spatula around the edge of each mold and dip the bases into very hot water for 2 seconds. Unmold each onto a plate and spoon the extra passion fruit pulp around the bases. Garnish with the halved strawberries and serve.

Serves 8

Note: Plan ahead with these, as they need to be refrigerated overnight. They are very quick to prepare.

Bread and butter pudding

¼ cup unsalted butter
8 thick slices day-old white bread
1 teaspoon ground cinnamon
2 tablespoons raisins
3 eggs
1 egg yolk
3 tablespoons sugar
1 cup milk
2 cups whipping cream
½ teaspoon vanilla extract
1 tablespoon raw sugar

Preheat the oven to 350°F. Melt 2 teaspoons of the butter and use to brush a 6-cup flameproof dish. Spread the bread very lightly with the remaining butter and cut each slice in half diagonally. Layer the bread in the prepared dish, sprinkling the cinnamon and raisins between each layer.

Lightly whisk together the eggs, egg yolk, and sugar in a large bowl. Heat the milk with the cream until just warm and stir in the vanilla. Whisk the cream mixture into the egg mixture. Strain the custard over the layered bread, then leave for 5 minutes before sprinkling with the raw sugar.

Bake for 30 minutes or until the custard has set and the bread is golden brown. Serve warm or at room temperature.

Serves 4

Raspberry mousse

2½ cups fresh or frozen raspberries, thawed
1²/₃ cups yogurt
1 tablespoon gelatin
2 egg whites
2 tablespoons sugar
raspberries, extra, to garnish

Mash the raspberries roughly with a fork. Combine in a large bowl with the yogurt.

Put 2 tablespoons hot water in a small heatproof bowl and sprinkle with the gelatin. Stand the bowl in a saucepan of very hot water and stir until the gelatin has dissolved and the mixture is smooth. Cool slightly, then whisk through the raspberry mixture.

Using an electric mixer, beat the egg whites in a clean, dry bowl until soft peaks form, then add the sugar, 1 tablespoon at a time, beating until dissolved. Gently fold through the berry mixture. Spoon into eight molds, and refrigerate for 2 hours or until set. Unmold onto a serving plate and serve with the extra raspberries.

Serves 8

Peaches poached in wine

4 ripe peaches
2 cups sauternes or other
  dessert white wine
1/4 cup orange liqueur
1 cinnamon stick
1 cup sugar
1 vanilla bean, split
8 fresh mint leaves
mascarpone or crème fraîche,
  to serve

Cut a small cross in the bottom of each peach. Immerse the peaches in boiling water for 30 seconds, then drain and cool slightly. Peel off the skin, cut in half, and remove the pits.

Place the wine, liqueur, cinnamon stick, sugar, and vanilla bean in a deep frying pan large enough to hold the peach halves in a single layer. Heat, stirring, until the sugar dissolves. Bring to a boil, then reduce the heat and simmer for 5 minutes. Add the peaches and simmer for 4 minutes, turning them halfway. Remove with a slotted spoon. Simmer the syrup for 6–8 minutes or until thick. Strain.

Arrange the peaches on a serving platter, cut-side up. Spoon the syrup over the top and garnish each half with a mint leaf. Serve the peaches warm or chilled, with a dollop of mascarpone or crème fraîche.

Serves 4

Mango ice cream in brandy snap baskets

3–4 mangoes
1/2 cup sugar
1/4 cup mango or apricot nectar
1 1/4 cups whipping cream
6 store-bought brandy snap baskets
mango slices, to garnish
fresh mint sprigs, to garnish

Purée the mango flesh in a food processor and chill. Place the chilled mango flesh in a large bowl and add the sugar and mango nectar. Stir for 1–2 minutes or until the sugar has dissolved.

Beat the cream in a bowl until stiff peaks form. Gently fold the cream into the mango mixture. Spoon the mixture into a deep tray or plastic container, cover, and freeze for 90 minutes or until half frozen. Quickly spoon the mixture into a food processor. Process for 30 seconds or until smooth. Return to the tray, cover, and freeze completely. Remove the ice cream from the freezer 10 minutes before serving to allow it to soften a little. To serve, place 2 scoops ice cream in each brandy snap basket and garnish with the mango slices and sprigs of mint.

Serves 6

Note: You have to allow for freezing time but preparation doesn't take very long. The ice cream should be frozen for at least 8 hours before serving and can be kept frozen for up to three weeks.

Chocolate croissant pudding

4 croissants, torn into pieces
3½ oz. dark chocolate, chopped
  into pieces
4 eggs
⅓ cup sugar
1 cup milk
1 cup whipping cream
½ teaspoon grated orange zest
⅓ cup orange juice
2 tablespoons coarsely chopped
  hazelnuts

Preheat the oven to 350°F. Grease the bottom and side of an 8-in. deep-sided cake pan and line the bottom of the pan with waxed paper.

Place the croissant pieces in the pan, then sprinkle evenly with chocolate.

Beat the eggs and sugar together until pale and creamy.

Heat the milk and cream in a saucepan to almost boiling, then remove from the heat. Gradually pour into the egg mixture, stirring constantly. Add the orange zest and juice and stir well.

Slowly pour the mixture over the croissants, allowing the liquid to be absorbed before adding more. Sprinkle the top with the hazelnuts and bake for 45 minutes or until a skewer comes out clean when inserted in the center.

Cool for 10 minutes. Run a knife around the edge, then unmold and invert. Cut into wedges and serve warm with whipped cream, if desired.

Serves 6–8

Coconut, ginger, and lime cake

2/3 cup unsalted butter, softened
3/4 cup sugar
2 teaspoons grated lime zest
2 eggs, lightly beaten
1/4 cup finely chopped glacé ginger
1 3/4 cups self-rising flour
1/2 cup dried coconut
3/4 cup milk

Preheat the oven to 350°F. Grease an 8 1/2 x 4 1/2-in. loaf pan and line the bottom with waxed paper. Beat the butter, sugar, and lime zest in a bowl with an electric mixer until pale and creamy.

Add the eggs gradually, beating well between each addition, then add the ginger. Fold in the sifted flour and the coconut alternately with the milk. Spoon the mixture into the prepared pan and smooth the surface. Bake for 50 minutes or until a skewer comes out clean when inserted into the center of the cake. Leave in the pan for 5 minutes, then unmold and invert onto a wire rack to cool. If desired, garnish with lime slices and lime zest and serve with ice cream.

Serves 8–10

Note: Prepare this delicious cake in a short time, then forget about it while it bakes to perfection.

Summer fruit compote

2 cups sugar
3 cups white wine, such
  as chardonnay
2 teaspoons finely grated lime zest
¼ cup lime juice
2 mangoes
3 peaches
3 nectarines
vanilla ice cream, to serve

Place the sugar, white wine, lime zest, and juice in a large saucepan. Stir over low heat for 3 minutes or until the sugar has dissolved. Bring to a boil, then reduce the heat and simmer for 2 minutes. Keep warm.

Cut the mangoes in half, then remove the skin. Cut each mango half into six thick wedges. Place the mango wedges in a large serving bowl. Cut a cross in one end of the peaches and nectarines and plunge them into a bowl of boiling water and then into cold water. Peel and cut into four wedges each, discarding the pits. Add to the mango wedges.

Pour the warm syrup over the fruit and refrigerate, covered, for 2–3 hours. To serve, return to room temperature and serve with ice cream.

Serves 6

Note: You can leave the peaches and nectarines unpeeled, if preferred. Don't forget to allow for the refrigeration time.

Strawberry ice cream with strawberry sauce

1 lb. strawberries, hulled, washed, and sliced
2 tablespoons sugar
2 tablespoons Cointreau or fresh orange juice
2 cups vanilla ice cream, slightly softened
3/4 cup blueberries, optional

Place the strawberries in a small saucepan, add the sugar and Cointreau, and cook over low heat for 5 minutes or until softened and the juices are released. Remove from the heat and refrigerate.

Place half the strawberry mixture in a food processor or blender and process for 20–30 seconds or until smooth. Spoon the ice cream into the food processor and process for 10 seconds or until well combined with the strawberry mixture. Pour into a rectangular pan and return to the freezer for 2–3 hours or until firm. Serve the ice cream with the remaining strawberry sauce and blueberries.

Serves 4

Plum crumble cake

¾ cup raw sugar
2 cups self-rising flour
⅔ cup unsalted butter
1 egg
2 15-oz. cans plums in syrup, drained
   and thinly sliced
1½ teaspoons ground cinnamon
⅔ cup blanched almonds, chopped

Preheat the oven to 350°F. Grease an 8-in. round pan and line the bottom with waxed paper. Blend the sugar, flour, and butter in a food processor in short bursts until the mixture is combined and crumbly.

Add the egg and process until well combined. Press half the mixture onto the bottom of the pan. Arrange the plum slices evenly over the dough, then sprinkle with the cinnamon.

Knead the almonds lightly into the remaining dough, then press onto the plum layer. Bake for 50 minutes or until a skewer comes out clean when inserted into the center of the cake. Leave in the pan for 15 minutes before carefully turning out onto a wire rack to cool slightly. Delicious served warm with whipped cream.

Serves 8

Winter fruit in orange ginger syrup

¼ cup sugar
¼ cup orange juice
2 strips orange peel
1 cinnamon stick
½ lb. dried fruit salad, large
  pieces cut in half
½ cup pitted dried dates
1 teaspoon grated fresh ginger
¾ cup low-fat, plain yogurt

Place the sugar, orange juice, orange peel, cinnamon stick, and 1½ cups water in a large saucepan. Stir over low heat until the sugar dissolves, then increase the heat and simmer, without stirring, for 5 minutes or until the syrup mixture has thickened slightly.

Add the dried fruit salad, dates, and ginger and toss well. Cover and simmer over low heat for 5 minutes or until the fruit has softened. Remove from the heat and set aside, covered, for 5 minutes. Discard the orange peel and cinnamon stick. If serving cold, remove from the saucepan and allow to cool.

Place the fruits in individual serving dishes, top with the yogurt, and drizzle a little of the syrup over the top. Serve immediately.

Serves 4

Mini passion fruit and almond cakes with lime curd

1/3 cup ground almonds
2 tablespoons all-purpose flour, sifted
3/4 cup confectioners' sugar, plus extra to dust
1 teaspoon finely grated lime zest
pulp from 1 passion fruit
1/2 cup unsalted butter, melted
2 eggs
2 tablespoons lime juice

Preheat the oven to 325°F. Lightly grease an 8-cup muffin pan. Place the ground almonds, flour, 1/2 cup confectioners' sugar, lime zest, passion fruit pulp, and half the butter in a bowl. Separate the eggs, reserve 1 egg yolk, and discard the other. Place the egg whites in a clean, dry bowl and beat to soft peaks. Gently fold into the almond mixture. Spoon into the prepared muffin pans and bake for 10–15 minutes or until the cakes are puffed and golden.

Meanwhile, place the lime juice, remaining butter, and remaining confectioners' sugar in a small saucepan, and heat to a simmer, stirring until all the sugar has dissolved. Remove from the heat and cool slightly, then whisk in the reserved egg yolk. Return to very low heat and stir for 5 minutes or until thickened. Do not boil.

Allow the cakes to rest in the pans for 5 minutes before gently removing. Serve two cakes per person, dusted with extra confectioners' sugar and drizzled with a little lime curd. Serve with cream or ice cream, if desired.

Serves 4

Note: Alternatively, the lime curd can be cooled and spread over the tops of the cakes.

Crème caramel

canola oil spray
1/3 cup sugar
1 1/2 cups nonfat milk
2 eggs
1 1/2 tablespoons sugar, extra
1/2 teaspoon vanilla extract
1 teaspoon maple syrup

Preheat the oven to 315°F. Lightly spray four 1/2-cup flameproof ramekins (5 in. diameter) with canola oil. Put the sugar and 1 1/2 tablespoons water in a small, heavy-bottomed saucepan. Stir over low heat until the sugar is dissolved. Bring to a boil, then reduce the heat and simmer until the syrup turns straw-colored and begins to caramelize. Remove from the heat and divide among the ramekins, coating the bottoms evenly.

Heat the milk in a small saucepan with a pinch of salt over low heat until almost boiling. Put the eggs and extra sugar in a bowl and whisk together for 2 minutes. Stir in the warm milk, vanilla, and maple syrup. Strain into a pitcher and divide among the ramekins.

Place the ramekins in a baking dish and add enough boiling water to reach halfway up the sides of the ramekins. Bake for 35 minutes or until the custards are set. Remove from the dish and allow to cool completely. Refrigerate for 2 hours or until chilled. To serve, carefully run a knife around the edge of each custard. Invert the ramekins onto plates and lift off, giving them a gentle shake.

Serves 4

Note: These can be served warm.

Lemon frozen yogurt

4 cups low-fat, vanilla yogurt
3/4 cup lemon juice
3/4 cup sugar
1/4 cup light corn syrup
1 teaspoon finely grated lemon zest
1/2 teaspoon vanilla extract

Place the yogurt in a fine strainer over a bowl and allow to drain in the refrigerator for at least 2 hours. Discard the liquid that drains off.

Place the remaining ingredients in a bowl and whisk together until the sugar dissolves. Add the drained yogurt and whisk in well.

If you have an ice-cream machine, pour the mixture into it and churn according to the manufacturer's instructions. Otherwise, place the mixture in a shallow metal tray and freeze for 2 hours or until the mixture is frozen around the edges. Transfer to a large bowl and beat until smooth. Repeat this step three times. For the final freezing, place in an airtight container, cover the surface with a piece of waxed paper and a lid, and freeze for 4 hours or overnight. Serve in parfait glasses.

Serves 6–8

Sand cake

¾ cup unsalted butter, softened
2 teaspoons vanilla extract
1 cup sugar
3 eggs
1½ cups self-rising flour
⅓ cup rice flour
⅓ cup milk

Preheat the oven to 350°F. Grease a 9-in. square pan and line the bottom with waxed paper.

Beat the butter, vanilla, sugar, eggs, flours, and milk with an electric mixer until combined, then beat at medium speed for 3 minutes or until thick and creamy.

Pour the mixture into the prepared pan and smooth the surface. Bake for 50 minutes or until a skewer comes out clean when inserted into the center of the cake. Leave for 10 minutes in the pan, then unmold and invert onto a wire rack to cool.

Serves 8–10

Individual sticky date cakes

1 1/2 cups pitted dates, chopped
1 teaspoon baking soda
2/3 cup unsalted butter, chopped
1 1/2 cups self-rising flour
1 1/4 cups firmly packed light
   brown sugar
2 eggs, lightly beaten
2 tablespoons golden syrup or dark
   corn syrup
3/4 cup whipping cream

Preheat the oven to 350°F. Grease six muffin cups. Place the dates and 1 cup water in a saucepan, bring to a boil, then remove from the heat and stir in the baking soda. Add 1/4 cup of the butter and stir until melted. Sift the flour into a large bowl, add 2/3 cup of the sugar, and stir. Make a well in the center, add the date mixture and egg, and stir until just combined. Spoon evenly into the muffin cups and bake for 20 minutes or until a skewer comes out clean when inserted into the center.

To make the sauce, place the golden syrup, cream, the remaining butter, and the remaining sugar in a small saucepan and stir over low heat for 3–4 minutes or until the sugar has dissolved. Bring to a boil, then reduce the heat and simmer, stirring occasionally, for 2 minutes. To serve, turn the cakes onto serving plates, pierce the cakes a few times with a skewer, and drizzle with the sauce. Serve with ice cream, if desired.

Makes 6

Dried apricot fool

1 oz. finely chopped glacé ginger
1 cup dried apricots, chopped
2 egg whites
2 tablespoons sugar
1 tablespoon shredded coconut,
  toasted

Place the ginger, apricots, and ⅓ cup water in a small saucepan. Cook, covered, over very low heat for 5 minutes, stirring occasionally. Remove from the heat and allow to cool completely.

Using an electric mixer, beat the egg whites in a clean, dry bowl until soft peaks form. Add the sugar and beat for 3 minutes or until thick and glossy. Quickly and gently fold the cooled apricot mixture into the egg mixture and divide among four chilled serving glasses. Sprinkle the coconut over the top and serve immediately.

Serves 4

Note: The apricots can scorch easily, so cook over low heat. Serve immediately or the egg white will slowly break down and lose volume.

No-bake chocolate squares

4 oz. shortbread cookies, roughly
  crushed
3/4 cup pistachios, shelled
1 cup hazelnuts, skinned
1/2 cup glacé cherries, roughly
  chopped
10 oz. semisweet chocolate
3/4 cup unsalted butter
1 teaspoon instant coffee grounds
2 eggs, lightly beaten

Toast the hazelnuts in a 350°F oven for 5–10 minutes or until golden. Transfer to a clean dishcloth and rub gently to remove the skins.

Lightly grease an 11 x 7-in. baking pan and line with waxed paper hanging over the two long sides. Combine the cookies, pistachios, 2/3 cup hazelnuts, and half the cherries.

Chop the chocolate and butter into small, evenly sized pieces and place in a heatproof bowl. Bring a saucepan of water to a boil and remove from the heat. Place the bowl over the pan, ensuring the bowl doesn't touch the water. Allow to rest, stirring once or twice, until the chocolate and butter have melted. Remove the bowl from the saucepan and when the mixture has cooled slightly, mix in the coffee and eggs. Pour over the nut mixture and mix well.

Pour the slice mixture into the pan and pat down well. Roughly chop the remaining hazelnuts and sprinkle the remaining cherries over the top. Refrigerate overnight.

Remove from the pan and trim the edges of the slice before cutting into pieces. Keep in the refrigerator.

Makes 18 pieces

Lemon granita

1 ¼ cups lemon juice
1 tablespoon lemon zest
¾ cup sugar

Place the lemon juice, lemon zest, and sugar in a small saucepan and stir over low heat for 5 minutes or until the sugar is dissolved. Remove from the heat and allow to cool.

Add 2 cups water to the juice mixture and mix together well. Pour the mixture into a shallow 12 x 8-in. metal container and place in the freezer until the mixture is beginning to freeze around the edges. Scrape the frozen sections back into the mixture with a fork. Repeat every 30 minutes until the mixture has evenly sized ice crystals. Beat the mixture with a fork just before serving. To serve, spoon the lemon granita into six chilled glasses.

Serves 6

Index

INDEX

INDEX

INDEX

Photographers: Cris Cordeiro, Craig Cranko, Joe Filshie, Ian Hofstetter, Tony Lyons, Andre Martin, Rob Reichenfeld, Brett Stevens

Food Stylists: Marie-Hélène Clauzon, Jane Collins, Sarah de Nardi, Georgina Dolling, Carolyn Fienberg, Mary Harris, Cherise Koch, Michelle Noerianto

Food Preparation: Alison Adams, Justine Johnson, Valli Little, Kate Murdoch, Briget Palmer, Justine Poole, Christine Sheppard, Angela Tregonning

Laurel Glen Publishing
An imprint of the Advantage Publishers Group
5880 Oberlin Drive, San Diego, CA 92121-4794
www.advantagebooksonline.com

All notations of errors or omissions should be addressed to Laurel Glen Publishing, editorial department, at the above address. All other correspondence (author inquiries, permissions, and rights) concerning the content of this book should be addressed to Murdoch Books®a division of Murdoch Magazines Pty Ltd, GPO Box 1203, Sydney NSW 2001, Australia.

NOTE: Those who might be at risk from the effects of salmonella poisoning (the elderly, pregnant women, young children, and those with a compromised immune system) should consult their physician before trying recipes made with raw eggs.

ISBN 1-57145-832-8
Library of Congress Cataloging-in-Publication Data available upon request.

Printed by Tien Wah Press, Singapore
1 2 3 4 5   06 05 04 03 02

Managing Editor: Rachel Carter
Editor: Wendy Stephen
Creative Director: Marylouise Brammer
Designer: Annette Fitzgerald
Food Director: Jane Lawson
Photographer (chapter openers): Ian Hofstetter
Stylist (chapter openers): Cherise Koch
Picture Librarian: Genevieve Huard
Chief Executive: Juliet Rogers
Publisher: Kay Scarlett
Production Manager: Kylie Kirkwood

Front cover: Fresh vegetable lasagna with arugula, page 78
Back cover: Eggplant, tomato, and goat cheese stacks, page 152
Spine: Mediterranean burgers, page 120